The Catechism of
Pope Saint Pius X

from an original text
published in Dublin in 1910

Distributed by:
ANGELUS PRESS
2918 Tracy Ave
Kansas City, MO 64109 USA
Order Line (800) 966-7337

Instauratio Press
Saint Benedict's Drive
Gladysdale Victoria, Australia

Cover picture:

Pope Saint Pius X

Extracted from **A Compendium of Catechetical Instruction**, edited by the Right Reverend Monsignor John Hagen, which was first published in Ireland in 1910.

This edition of part of the above work was published in June 1993

Instauratio Press
Saint Benedict's Drive
Gladysdale Vic. 3797
Australia

The typography of this book is the property of **Instauratio Press.** Apart from any fair dealing for the purpose of private study, criticism or review, as permitted under the Copyright Act, no part may be reproduced by any process without permission in writing from the publisher.

ISBN 0 646 14292 5

Contents

Introduction

Foreword	vii
Introduction to **A Compendium of Catechetical Instruction** edited by	
The Right Reverend Monsignor John Hagen	x

Preliminary Lesson

On Christian Doctrine and its Principal Parts	1

The Apostles' Creed

The Creed in General	5
The First Article of the Creed	6
God the Father Almighty	6
On the Creation	7
The Angels	8
Man	10
The Second Article of the Creed	14
The Third Article of the Creed	16
The Fourth Article of the Creed	18
The Fifth Article of the Creed	21
The Sixth Article of the Creed	22
The Seventh Article of the Creed	23
The Eighth Article of the Creed	25
The Ninth Article of the Creed	27
The Church in General	27
The Church in Particular	28
The Church Teaching and the Church Taught	33
The Pope and the Bishops	35
The Ninth Article of the Creed	38

The Communion of Saints	38
Those Outside the Communion of Saints	41
The Tenth Article of the Creed	42
The Eleventh Article of the Ccreed	43
The Twelfth Article of the Creed	44

Prayer

Prayer in General	47
The Lord's Prayer	51
The Lord's Prayer in General	51
The First Petition	52
The Second Petition	53
The Third Petition	54
The Fourth Petition	55
The Fifth Petition	56
The Sixth Petition	57
The Seventh Petition	57
The Hail Mary	59

The Sacraments

Nature of the Sacraments	63
The Principal Effect of the Sacraments : Grace	64
The Character Impressed by some of the Sacraments	67
Baptism	68
Nature and Effects of Baptism	68
Minister of Baptism	69
The Rite of Baptism and the Disposition of the Adult who Receives It	69
Necessity of Baptism and the Obligations of the Baptised	71
Names and Sponsors	72
Chrism or Confirmation	73
The Blessed Eucharist	76
The Nature of this Sacrament—The Real Presence	76

The Institution and Effects of the Sacrament of the Eucharist	80
The Dispositions necessary to Receive Holy Communion worthily	81
The Way to Go to Communion	84
The Precept of Holy Communion	85
The Holy Sacrifice of the Mass	86
The Essence, Institution and Ends of the Holy Sacrifice of the Mass	86
The Way to Assist at Mass	89
The Sacrament of Penance	91
Penance in General	91
The Effects and the Necessity of the Sacrament of Penance and the Dispositions to Receive It Properly	94
Examination of Conscience	95
Sorrow	96
Resolution of Sinning No More	101
The Accusation of Sins to the Confessor	102
How to Make a Good Confession	106
Absolution	107
Satisfaction or Penance	109
Indulgences	112
The Sacrament of Extreme Unction	114
The Sacrament of Holy Orders	116
The Sacrament of Matrimony	119
Nature of the Sacrament of Matrimony	119
Minister—Rite—Dispositions	120
Conditions and Impediments	122

The Commandments of God and of the Church

The Commandments of God in General	125
The First Commandment	126
The Second Commandment	130
The Third Commandment	133

The Fourth Commandment	134
The Fifth Commandment	137
The Sixth and Ninth Commandments	139
The Seventh Commandment	140
The Eighth Commandment	143
The Tenth Commandment	145
The Precepts of the Church in General	**146**
The First Precept of the Church	147
The Second Precept of the Church	149
The Third Precept of the Church	152
The Fourth Precept of the Church	154
The Fifth Precept of the Church	154

On the Virtues and Vices

The Main Virtues	**157**
Theological Virtues	157
On Faith	158
The Mysteries of Faith	159
On Holy Scripture	159
On Tradition.	162
On Hope	162
On Charity	163
On The Cardinal Virtues	165
The Gifts of the Holy Ghost	**166**
The Beatitudes	**167**
The Works of Mercy	**170**
The Main Kinds of Sins	**171**
The Vices and Other Very Grievous Sins	**173**
The Last Ends and other Principal Means to avoid Sin	**174**
Pious Exercises Recommended for each Day	**175**

Foreword

In these times of Catechetical disarray, there is an even greater need to have available the Catholic Doctrine in a concise, precise and reliable authoritative form. In the first half of this century, the Catholic Bishops of each country had developed their own excellent Catechisms: these included the **Penny Catechism** in England, the **Baltimore Catechism** in the United States, the **Green Catechism** in Australia, the *Catéchisme des diocèses de France* in France, and many more. Yet none of these approach the completeness and beauty of St. Pius X's own Catechism, which preceded them all.

After the Second Vatican Council, a number of new catechisms appeared which did not present Catholic Doctrine as it should be presented, and these new publications even included some very grave errors. Coupled with the new methods, whereby children are not required to memorise, two generations of children have grown up not knowing the Catholic Faith. For many years Rome did nothing. Now there has been published the new **Catechism of the Catholic Church**, as I write, still available only in French, the language in which it was written. It has been written for Bishops, who are required to adapt it to the needs of the faithful. One may fear that some Bishops will put off this task for a very long time, others will water-down the Doctrine even further; yet others will give only a partial presentation of the Doctrine, leaving important points untold.

Thus the need is still great for a Catechism to be put in the hands of the student in which he may find clear and complete answers to his questions. What better could be given him than the **Catechism of St. Pius X**, the holy Pope of the modern era? This present edition contains the text of the Larger Catechism. It is ideal as a text book for high school students.

To my knowledge, the Catechism of St. Pius X has never been published in English in its original text. There is one **Catechism of Christian Doctrine**, published by the Rev. Msgr. Eugene Kevane in Virginia, USA in 1974, but in fact, it contains a much later text which lacks much of the original text: it is the translation of the *Catechismo della Dottrina Cristiana*, the standard Italian Catechism, as it was in 1953. That Italian Catechism is in turn, a summary and reduction of the original Catechism of St. Pius X. The American edition in 1974 has further been "adapted according to the Second Vatican Council", thus losing much of the value of the original text (e.g. expressions like "Soldiers of Christ" are suppressed from the teaching on the effects of Confirmation). The only book where I was able to find the authentic text is the excellent **Compendium of Catechetical Instruction** by the Right Reverend Monsignor John Hagan, first published in Dublin in 1910, and containing for each chapter of the Catechism the relevant part from the **Catechism of the Council of Trent**, the questions and answers of the Catechism of Saint Pius X and Father Raineri's **Catechetical Instructions**, which were very popular in the nineteenth century.

We present here Msgr. Hagan's text with very slight modifications of style only. The current discipline of the Church on matters such as fasting has been included in smaller print to bring the text up-to-date without altering the original answers.

It is to be noted that though the Catechism of the Council of Trent has four parts, the Creed, the Sacraments, the Commandments and Prayer, the Catechism of St. Pius X puts prayer as the second part and adds a fifth part on "Virtues and other things which a Christian should know." This extra place given to prayer is worth noting: the knowledge of God leads us to prayer; for without prayer, we could not receive the fruits of the Sacraments; with the grace of Christ received by prayer and the

Sacraments, we can fulfil the Commandments; guided by the Commandments, we build virtues and avoid sin.

May this edition of Saint Pius X's Catechism help priests, teachers and parents to impart the knowledge and love of the Doctrine of the Catholic Church to their pupils and their children in all its entirety and beauty. It is our hope that it will also help adult Catholics to revise and deepen their own knowledge of the Faith. It will be very helpful to catechumens to assist them towards a complete knowledge of the one true Faith. May the clear knowledge of the eternal truths of our Faith build in all readers the great certitudes that are the foundations of solid virtues. May the Immaculate Heart of the Blessed Virgin Mary obtain all these graces for the readers of this volume, and may they pray for me.

Father François Laisney
Sydney
Feast of the Purification of Our Lady, 1993.

Introduction to "A Compendium of Catechetical Instruction" by the Right Reverend Monsignor John Hagan

The Catechism, as we now know it, is of comparatively recent origin. Previous to the invention of printing, and the consequent possibility of the spread of books and education among the masses of the people, the widespread use of a Catechism was plainly out of the question. Its place was supplied by brief formulae, not infrequently set to rhyme, which were committed to memory and handed down from generation to generation, conveying a brief statement of the truths more necessary to salvation. The nearest approaches to the modern Catechism would be St. Cyril's Catechesis, St. Augustine's Instruction of the Ignorant, and, later on, certain works of Alcuin, Rabanus Maurus, and Gerson.

The publication and widespread diffusion of an infinity of Catechisms compiled by Luther and his followers for the purpose of disseminating their new doctrines, stimulated the energies of Catholic writers in a similar direction; and accordingly several Catholic Catechisms were issued within the next few years giving a clear and simple statement of Catholic doctrine, particularly on those points that were being attacked by the reformers. Of these, several of which were prescribed for diocesan use, the principal were those of Erasmus, Witzel, Dietenberg, Fabri, Titelmann, Hosius, and Blessed Peter Canisius, in Germany; of Parvi, de Bourbon, du Bellay, de Thou, in France; of Sonnius, Hessel, and Hunnaeus, in the Low Countries; of Dominic Soto, John of St Thomas, and Florez, in Spain; of Bartholomew of the Martyrs and Louis of Granada in Portugal; and of Cardinal Contarini, Marini, and Crispoldi, in Italy.

But, as already pointed out, the Fathers of the Council of Trent showed at a very early date that they were satisfied with none of the existing works, and that they were fully alive to the need and necessity of preparing an authoritative Catechism. The realisation of their desire, however, was retarded for several years by events over which they had little control; and when the work was finally taken in hand another idea prevailed, resulting in the publication of a manual for the use of the clergy, and not, as originally suggested, a Catechism for children and uninstructed adults.

Of the countless Catechisms that continued to appear, two—those of Bellarmine and Canisius—have steadily held their ground ever since, and to a large extent have served as the models of nearly all subsequent compilations of the kind. The influence of Canisius, however, has on the whole been limited to Germany; whereas Bellarmine's Catechism, which was written by command of Pope Clement VIII in 1597, has been copied in almost every other country in the world. At an early date it was translated into Arabic, Latin, Modern Greek, French, Spanish, German, English, and Polish. It had the warm approbation of Clement VIII, who prescribed it for use in the Papal States; of Urban VIII, who directed it to be adopted in all the Eastern missions; of Innocent XIII and Benedict XIV; particularly of the very important Council of all Italy, held at Rome, in 1725, which made it obligatory in all the dioceses of the peninsula; and finally of the Vatican Council,[1] which indicated it as the model for a proposed universal Catechism.

Though Bellarmine's Catechism was largely followed as a model all over the world, yet, owing to the modifications introduced in diocesan editions, it came to pass in the course of time that almost every diocese had its own Catechism, differing in many respects from the Catechisms of other dioceses.

The obvious inconvenience of this bewildering multiplicity of Catechisms occupied the attention of the Fathers of the Vatican Council,[2] the great majority of whom were agreed as to the desirability of having a uniform small Catechism for the faithful all over the world. Early during the sittings of the Council, forty-one of the assembled Fathers devoted six sessions (February 10 to February 22) to an examination of the question; and the report which they drew up occupied the attention of the whole Council during the sittings of April 29 and 30. The question being put to a vote on May 4, an immense majority was found to be in favour of the compilation of a small uniform Catechism, to be compiled in Latin,

1 The First Vatican Council
2 The First Vatican Council.

translated into every language, and made obligatory in every diocese. But the approach of the Italian troops towards the walls of Rome brought the Council to an untimely end and there was no time to promulgate the constitution on the proposed uniform Catechism, so that it has not the force of law.

The idea, however, has never been lost sight of. During the sitting of the first Catechetical Congress in 1880, the then Bishop of Mantua (later St. Pius X) proposed that the Holy Father be petitioned to arrange for the compilation of a simple, plain, brief, and popular Catechism for uniform use all over the world. Shortly after his elevation to the Chair of Peter, Pius X at once set about realising, within certain limits, his own proposal of 1880, by prescribing a uniform Catechism—the Compendium of Christian Doctrine—for use in the dioceses of the ecclesiastical province of Rome, at the same time indicating that it was his earnest desire to have the same manual adopted all over Italy. The text selected was, with slight modifications, that which had been adopted for some years by the united hierarchy of Piedmont, Liguria, Lombardy, Emilia, and Tuscany.

It contains three Catechisms. The first, which is intended for infant schools and for the home, and which covers about thirteen pages, sets forth briefly the more elementary truths of faith, chiefly by way of formulae to be committed to memory. The second part, called the Short Catechism, is intended chiefly for primary schools and for children preparing for the sacraments. It contains about sixty pages devoted to a brief exposition of the doctrine of the Creed, Sacraments, Commandments, and Prayer. The Larger Catechism, which forms the third part, explains these at greater length in about 200 pages. It is succeeded by an explanation of the principal feasts of the year, covering sixty pages, followed by forty pages of a Brief History of Religion, and concludes with a certain number of daily prayers, and prayers for special occasions.[3]

J.H.
Irish College, Rome
Feast of Saint Charles Borromeo, 1911.

---

3   Msgr Hagen is here describing the contents of his **Compendium of Catechetical Instruction**. What is published in this volume is 'The Larger Catechism'.

Preliminary Lesson

On Christian Doctrine and its Principal Parts

1 Q. Are you a Christian?
A. Yes, I am a Christian, by the grace of God.

2 Q. Why do you say: *By the grace of God?*
A. I say: *By the grace of God,* because to be a Christian is a perfectly gratuitous gift of God, which we ourselves could not have merited.

3 Q. Who is a true Christian?
A. A true Christian is he who is baptised, who believes and professes the Christian Doctrine, and obeys the lawful pastors of the Church.

4 Q. What is Christian Doctrine?
A. Christian doctrine is the doctrine which Jesus Christ our Lord taught us to show us the way of salvation.

5 Q. Is it necessary to learn the doctrine taught by Jesus Christ?
A. It certainly is necessary to learn the doctrine taught by Jesus Christ, and those who fail to do so are guilty of a grave breach of duty.

6 Q. Are parents and guardians bound to send their children and those dependent on them to catechism?
A. Parents and guardians are bound to see that their children and dependents learn Christian Doctrine, and they are guilty before God if they neglect this duty.

7 Q. From whom are we to receive and learn Christian Doctrine?
A. We are to receive and learn Christian Doctrine from the Holy Catholic Church.

8 Q. How are we certain that the Christian Doctrine which we receive from the Holy Catholic Church is really true?
A. We are certain that the doctrine which we receive from the Holy Catholic Church is true, because Jesus Christ, the divine Author of this doctrine, committed it through His Apostles to the Church, which He founded and made the infallible teacher of all men, promising her His divine assistance until the end of time.

9 Q. Are there other proofs of the truth of Christian Doctrine?
A. The truth of Christian Doctrine is also shown by the eminent sanctity of numbers who have professed it and who still profess it, by the heroic fortitude of the martyrs, by its marvellous and rapid propagation in the world, and by its perfect preservation throughout so many centuries of ceaseless and varied struggles.

10 Q. What and how many are the principal and most necessary parts of Christian Doctrine?
A. The principal and most necessary parts of Christian Doctrine are four: The Creed, The Our Father, The Commandments, and The Sacraments.

11 Q. What does the Creed teach us?
A. The Creed teaches us the principal articles of our holy faith.

12 Q. What does the *Our Father* teach us?
A. The *Our Father* teaches us all that we are to hope from God, and all we are to ask of Him.

13 Q. What do the Commandments teach us?
A. The Commandments teach us all that we are to do to please God—all of which is summed up in loving God above all things and our neighbour as ourselves for the love of God.

14 Q. What does the doctrine of the Sacraments teach us?
A. The doctrine of the Sacraments shows us the nature and right use of those means which Jesus Christ has instituted to remit our sins, give us His grace, infuse into and increase in us the virtues of faith, hope, and charity.

The Apostles' Creed

The Creed in General

1 Q. What is the first part of Christian Doctrine?
A. The first part of Christian Doctrine is the Symbol of the Apostles, commonly called the Creed.

2 Q. Why do you call the Creed the Symbol of the Apostles?
A. The Creed is called the Symbol of the Apostles because it is a summary of the truths of faith taught by the Apostles.

3 Q. How many articles are there in the Creed?
A. There are twelve articles in the Creed.

4 Q. Recite them.
- (1) I believe in God, the Father Almighty, Creator of heaven and earth;
- (2) And in Jesus Christ, His only Son, our Lord;
- (3) Who was conceived by the Holy Ghost; born of the Virgin Mary;
- (4) Suffered under Pontius Pilate: was crucified, dead, and buried;
- (5) He descended into hell: the third day He rose again from the dead;
- (6) He ascended into Heaven: sitteth at the right hand of God the Father Almighty;
- (7) From thence He shall come to judge the living and the dead.
- (8) I believe in the Holy Ghost;
- (9) The Holy Catholic Church; the Communion of Saints;
- (10) The forgiveness of sins;
- (11) The resurrection of the body;
- (12) Life everlasting. Amen.

5 Q. What is meant by the word: *I believe*, which you say at the beginning of the Symbol?
A. The word: *I believe*, means I hold everything that is contained in these twelve articles to be perfectly true; and I believe these truths more firmly than if I saw them with my eyes, because God, who can neither deceive nor be deceived, has revealed them to the Holy Catholic Church and through this Church to us.

6 Q. What do the articles of the Creed contain?
A. The articles of the Creed contain the principal truths to be believed concerning God, Jesus Christ, and the Church, His Spouse.

7 Q. Is it useful to recite the Creed frequently?
A. It is most useful to recite the Creed frequently, so as to impress the truths of faith more and more deeply on our hearts.

The First Article of the Creed

God the Father Almighty

1 Q. What does the First Article of the Creed: *I believe in God, the Father Almighty, Creator of heaven and earth,* teach us?
A. The First Article of the Creed teaches us that there is one God, and only one; that He is omnipotent and has created heaven and earth and all things contained in them, that is to say, the whole Universe.

2 Q. How do we know that there is a God?
A. We know that there is a God because reason proves it and faith confirms it.

3 Q. Why do we call God the Father?
A. We call God the Father because by nature He is the Father of

the Second Person of the Blessed Trinity, that is to say, of the Son begotten of Him; because God is the Father of all men, whom He has created and whom He preserves and governs; finally, because by grace He is the Father of all good Christians, who are hence called the adopted sons of God.

4 Q. Why is the Father the First Person of the Blessed Trinty?

A. The Father is the First Person of the Blessed Trinity, because He does not proceed from any other Person, but is the Principle of the other two Persons, that is, of the Son and of the Holy Ghost.

5 Q. What is meant by the word Omnipotent?
A. The word Omnipotent means that God can do all that He wills.

6 Q. God can neither sin nor die, how then do we say He can do all things?
A. Though He can neither sin nor die, we say God can do all things, because to be able to sin or die is not an effect of power, but of weakness which cannot exist in God who is most perfect.

On the Creation

7 Q. What is meant by the words: *Creator of heaven and earth?*
A. To create means to make out of nothing; hence, God is called the Creator of heaven and of earth, because He made heaven and earth and all things contained therein, that is, the whole Universe, out of nothing.

8 Q. Was the world created by the Father alone?
A. The world was created by all the Three Divine Persons, because whatever one Person does with regard to creatures is done by the other two Persons in one and the selfsame act.

9 Q. Why then is creation specially attributed to the Father?
A. Creation is specially attributed to the Father because creation is a work of Divine Omnipotence, which is specially attributed to the Father, just as wisdom is attributed to the Son, and goodness to the Holy Ghost, though all three Persons possess the same Omnipotence, Wisdom, and Goodness.

10 Q. Does God take any interest in the world and in the things created by Him?
A. Yes, God takes an interest in the world and in all things created by Him; He preserves them, and governs them by His infinite goodness and wisdom; and nothing happens here below that He does not either will or permit.

11 Q. Why do you say that nothing happens here below that He does not either will or permit?
A. We say that nothing happens here below that He does not either will or permit, because there are some things which God wills and commands, while there are others which He simply does not prevent, such as sin.

12 Q. Why does not God prevent sin?
A. God does not prevent sin, because even from the very abuse man makes of the liberty with which He is endowed, God knows how to bring forth good and to make His mercy or His justice become more and more resplendent.

The Angels

13 Q. Which are the noblest of God's creatures?
A. The noblest creatures created by God are the Angels.

14 Q. Who are the Angels?
A. The Angels are intelligent and purely spiritual creatures.

The Apostles Creed

15 Q. Why did God create the Angels?
A. God created the Angels so as to be honoured and served by them, and to give them eternal happiness.

16 Q. What form and figure have the Angels?
A. The Angels have neither form nor material figure of any kind, because they are pure spirits created by God in such a way as to exist without having to be united to a body.

17 Q. Why then are the angels represented under sensible forms?
A. The Angels are represented under sensible forms:
  (1) As a help to our imagination;
  (2) Because they have thus appeared many times to men, as we read in Sacred Scripture.

18 Q. Were all the angels faithful to God?
A. No, the Angels were not all faithful to God, many of them through pride claimed to be His equals and independent of Him—for which sin they were banished for ever from Paradise and condemned to hell.

19 Q. What are the Angels called who were banished for ever from Paradise and condemned to hell?
A. The Angels banished for ever from Paradise and condemned to hell are called demons, and their chief is called Lucifer or Satan.

20 Q. Can the demons do us any harm?
A. Yes, the demons can do us great harm both in soul and body, especially by tempting us to sin, provided God permits them to do so.

21 Q. Why do they tempt us?
A. The demons tempt us because of the envy they bear us, which makes them desire our eternal damnation; and because of their hatred of God, whose image is reflected in us. God on the

other hand permits these temptations in order that we may overcome them by His grace, and thus practise virtue and acquire merit for Heaven.

22 Q. How are temptations conquered?
A. Temptations are conquered by watchfulness, prayer and Christian mortification.

23 Q. What are the angels called who remained faithful to God?
A. The Angels who remained faithful to God are called the good Angels, heavenly Spirits, or simply Angels.

24 Q. What became of the Angels who remained faithful to God?
A. The Angels who remained faithful to God were confirmed in grace, for ever enjoy the vision of God, love Him, bless Him, and praise Him eternally.

25 Q. Does God use the Angels as His ministers?
A. Yes, God uses the Angels as His ministers, and especially does He entrust to many of them the office of acting as our guardians and protectors.

26 Q. Should we have a particular devotion to our Guardian Angel?
A. Yes, we should have a particular devotion to our Guardian Angel; we should honour him, invoke his aid, follow his inspirations, and be grateful to him for the continual assistance he affords us.

Man

27 Q. Which is the noblest creature God has placed on earth?
A. The noblest creature God has placed on earth is man.

The Apostles Creed

28 Q. What is man?
A. Man is a rational creature composed of soul and body.

29 Q. What is the soul?
A. The soul is the noblest part of man, because it is a spiritual substance, endowed with intelligence and will, capable of knowing God and of possessing Him for all eternity.

30 Q. Can the human soul be seen and touched?
A. Our soul can neither be seen nor touched, because it is a spirit.

31 Q. Does the human soul die with the body?
A. The human soul never dies; faith and our very reason prove that it is immortal.

32 Q. Is man free in his actions?
A. Yes, man is free in his actions and each one feels within himself that he can do a thing or leave it undone, or do one thing rather than another.

33 Q. Explain human liberty by an example.
A. If I voluntarily tell a lie, I know that I could have left it unsaid or that I could have remained silent, and that, on the other hand, I could also speak differently and tell the truth.

34 Q. Why do we say that man was created to the image and likeness of God?
A. We say that man was created to the image and likeness of God because the human soul is spiritual and rational, free in its operations, capable of knowing and loving God and of enjoying Him for ever—perfections which reflect a ray of the infinite greatness of the Lord in us.

35 Q. In what state did God place our first parents, Adam and Eve?
A. God placed our first parents, Adam and Eve, in the state of innocence and grace; but they soon fell away by sin.

36 Q. Besides innocence and sanctifying grace did God confer any other gifts on our first parents?
A. Besides innocence and sanctifying grace, God conferred on our first parents other gifts, which, along with sanctifying grace, they were to transmit to their descendants; these were:
    (1) Integrity, that is, the perfect subjection of sense to reason;
    (2) Immortality;
    (3) Immunity from all pain and sorrow;
    (4) A knowledge in keeping with their state.

37 Q. What was the nature of Adam's sin?
A. Adam's sin was a sin of pride and of grave disobedience.

38 Q. What chastisement was meted out to the sin of Adam and Eve?
A. Adam and Eve lost the grace of God and the right they had to Heaven; they were driven out of the earthly Paradise, subjected to many miseries of soul and body, and condemned to death.

39 Q. If Adam and Eve had not sinned, would they have been exempt from death?
A. If Adam and Eve had not sinned and if they had remained faithful to God, they would, after a happy and tranquil sojourn here on earth, and without dying, have been transferred by God into Heaven, to enjoy a life of unending glory.

40 Q. Were these gifts due to man?
A. These gifts were in no way due to man, but were absolutely gratuitous and supernatural; and hence, when Adam disobeyed the divine command, God could without any injustice deprive both Adam and his posterity of them.

41 Q. Is this sin proper to Adam alone?
A. This sin is not Adam's sin alone, but it is also our sin,

The Apostles Creed

though in a different sense. It is Adam's sin because he committed it by an act of his will, and hence in him it was a personal sin. It is our sin also because Adam, having committed it in his capacity as the head and source of the human race, it was transmitted by natural generation to all his descendants: and hence in us it is original sin.

42 Q. How is it possible for original sin to be transmitted to all men?
A. Original sin is transmitted to all men because God, having conferred sanctifying grace and other supernatural gifts on the human race in Adam, on the condition that Adam should not disobey Him; and Adam having disobeyed, as head and father of the human race, rendered human nature rebellious against God. And hence, human nature is transmitted to all the descendants of Adam in a state of rebellion against God, and deprived of divine grace and other gifts.

43 Q. Do all men contract original sin?
A. Yes, all men contract original sin, with the exception of the Blessed Virgin, who was preserved from it by a singular privilege of God, in view of the merits of Jesus Christ our Saviour.

44 Q. Could not men be saved after Adam's sin?
A. After Adam's sin men could not be saved, if God had not shown mercy towards them.

45 Q. What was the mercy shown by God to the human race?
A. The mercy shown by God to the human race was that of immediately promising Adam a divine Redeemer or Messiah, and of sending this Messiah in His own good time to free men from the slavery of sin and of the devil.

46 Q. Who is the promised Messiah?
A. The promised Messiah is Jesus Christ, as the Second Article of the Creed teaches.

The Second Article of the Creed

1 Q. What are we taught in the Second Article: *And in Jesus Christ His only Son our Lord?*
A. The Second Article of the Creed teaches us that the Son of God is the Second Person of the Blessed Trinity; that, like the Father, He is God eternal, omnipotent, Creator and Lord; that He became man to save us; and that the Son of God, made man, is called Jesus Christ.

2 Q. Why is the Second Person called the Son?
A. The Second Person is called the Son, because He is begotten by the Father from all eternity by way of intelligence; and for this reason He is also called the Eternal Word of the Father.

3 Q. Since we also are sons of God, why is Jesus Christ called the only Son of God the Father?
A. Jesus Christ is called the only Son of God the Father, because He alone is His Son by nature, whereas we are His sons by creation and adoption.

4 Q. Why is Jesus Christ called our Lord?
A. Jesus Christ is called our Lord, because, not only did He as God, together with the Father and the Holy Ghost, create us; but He has also as God and Man redeemed us.

5 Q. Why is the Son of God, made man, called *Jesus?*
A. The Son of God, made man, is called *Jesus*, that is to say, Saviour, because He has saved us from the eternal death merited by our sins.

6 Q. Who gave the name of Jesus to the Son of God, made man?
A. The Eternal Father Himself, through the Archangel Gabriel, gave the name of Jesus to the Son of God made man, at the moment when the Archangel announced to the Blessed Virgin the mystery of the Incarnation.

The Apostles Creed

7 Q. Why is the Son of God made man also called *Christ?*
A. The Son of God made man is also called *Christ,* that is to say, anointed or consecrated, because kings, priests and prophets were anointed of old; and Jesus is the King of kings, High Priest, and supreme Prophet.

8 Q. Was Jesus Christ really anointed and consecrated with a material anointing?
A. The anointing of Jesus Christ was not material, like that of the kings, priests and prophets of old, but wholly spiritual and divine, because the fullness of the Divinity dwells in Him substantially.

9 Q. Had men any idea of Jesus Christ previous to His coming?
A. Yes, previous to His coming men had some idea of Jesus Christ in the promise of the Messiah, which God made to our first parents, Adam and Eve, and which He renewed to the holy Patriarchs; and also in the prophecies and the many figures which foreshadowed Him.

10 Q. How do we know that Jesus Christ is truly the Messiah and Promised Redeemer?
A. We know that Jesus Christ is truly the Messiah and Promised Redeemer from the fact that in Him are verified:
    (1) All that the prophecies foretold,
    (2) And all that the figures of the Old Testament fore shadowed.

11 Q. What did the prophecies foretell of the Redeemer?
A. Regarding the Redeemer, the prophecies foretold the tribe and the family from which He was to come; the place and time of His birth; His miracles and the most minute circumstances of His Passion and Death; His Resurrection and Ascension into heaven; and His spiritual, perpetual and universal Kingdom, that is, the Holy Catholic Church.

12 Q. Which are the principal figures of the Redeemer in the Old Testament?
A. The principal figures of the Redeemer in the Old Testament are: the innocent Abel; the High Priest Melchisedech; the sacrifice of Isaac; Joseph sold by his brethren; the prophet Jonas; the Paschal Lamb; and the Brazen Serpent set up by Moses in the desert.

13 Q. How do you know that Jesus Christ is true God?
A. We know that Jesus Christ is true God:
  (1) From the testimony of the Father saying: This is My beloved Son in whom I am well pleased, hear ye Him;
  (2) From the attestation of Jesus Christ Himself, confirmed by the most stupendous miracles;
  (3) From the teaching of the Apostles;
  (4) From the unvarying tradition of the Catholic Church.

14 Q. Mention the chief miracles wrought by Jesus Christ?
A. Besides His Resurrection, the chief miracles wrought by Jesus Christ are; the restoring of health to the sick, of sight to the blind, of hearing to the deaf, and of life to the dead.

The Third Article of the Creed

1 Q. What is taught in the Third Article: *Who was conceived by the Holy Ghost, born of the Virgin Mary?*
A. The Third Article of the Creed teaches that by the operation of the Holy Ghost the Son of God took a body and soul like ours, in the chaste womb of the Virgin Mary, and that He was born of that Virgin.

2 Q. Did the Father and the Son also take part in forming the body and creating the soul of Jesus Christ?
A. Yes, the whole Three divine Persons co-operated in forming the body and in creating the soul of Jesus Christ.

The Apostles Creed

3 Q. Why then is it simply said: *He was conceived by the Holy Ghost?*
A. It is simply said: *He was conceived by the Holy Ghost,* because the Incarnation of the Son of God is a work of goodness and love, and the works of goodness and love are attributed to the Holy Ghost.

4 Q. In becoming man did the Son of God cease to be God?
A. No, the Son of God became man without ceasing to be God.

5 Q. Jesus Christ, then, is God and man at the same time?
A. Yes, the incarnate Son of God, that is, Jesus Christ, is both God and man, perfect God and perfect man.

6 Q. Are there, then, two natures in Jesus Christ?
A. Yes, in Jesus Christ, who is both God and man, there are two natures, the divine and the human.

7 Q. In Jesus Christ are there also two Persons, the divine and the human?
A. No, in the Son of God made man there is only one Person, namely, the divine.

8 Q. How many wills are there in Jesus Christ?
A. In Jesus Christ there are two wills, the one divine, the other human.

9 Q. Did Jesus Christ possess free will?
A. Yes, Jesus Christ possessed free will, but He could not do evil, since to be able to do evil is a defect, and not a perfection, of liberty.

10 Q. Are the Son of God and the Son of Mary one and the same Person?
A. Yes, the Son of God and the Son of Mary are one and the same Person, that is, Jesus Christ, true God and true man.

11 Q. Is the Blessed Virgin the Mother of God?
A. Yes, the Blessed Virgin is the Mother of God, because she is the Mother of Jesus Christ, who is true God.

12 Q. How did Mary become the Mother of Jesus Christ?
A. Mary became the Mother of Jesus Christ solely through the operation and power of the Holy Ghost.

13 Q. Is it of faith that Mary was always a Virgin?
A. Yes, it is of faith that the most holy Mary was always a Virgin, and she is called the Virgin of virgins.

The Fourth Article of the Creed

1 Q. What are we taught in the Fourth Article: *Suffered under Pontius Pilate, was crucified, dead, and buried?*
A. The Fourth Article of the Creed teaches us that to redeem the world by His Precious Blood Jesus Christ suffered under Pontius Pilate, the Governor of Judea, died on the tree of the Cross, and, on being taken down therefrom, was buried.

2 Q. What does the word *suffered* denote?
A. The word *suffered* denotes all the pains endured by Jesus Christ during His Passion.

3 Q. Did Jesus Christ suffer as God or as man?
A. Jesus Christ suffered as man alone; as God He could neither suffer nor die.

4 Q. What class of punishment was that of the Cross?
A. The punishment of the Cross in those days was the cruellest and the most ignominious of all punishments.

5 Q. Who was it that condemned Jesus Christ to be crucified?
A. He who condemned Jesus Christ to be crucified was Pontius Pilate, the Governor of Judea who, though recognising His in-

nocence, cravenly yielded to the threats of the people of Jerusalem.

6 Q. Could not Jesus Christ have freed Himself from the hands of Pilate and the Jews?
A. Yes, Jesus Christ could have freed Himself from the hands of Pilate and the Jews, but knowing it was His Eternal Father's will that He should suffer and die for our salvation, He voluntarily submitted; nay, He Himself went forth to meet His enemies and freely permitted Himself to be taken and led to death.

7 Q. Where was Jesus Christ crucified?
A. Jesus Christ was crucified on Mount Calvary.

8 Q. What did Jesus Christ do while on the Cross?
A. On the Cross Jesus Christ prayed for His enemies; gave His own Most Blessed Mother as a Mother to St. John, and, in his person, to all of us; offered up His death in sacrifice; and satisfied the justice of God for the sins of men.

9 Q. Would it not have been enough for an Angel to come and make satisfaction for us?
A. No, it would not have been enough for an Angel to come and make satisfaction for us, because the offence given to God by sin was, in a certain sense, infinite, and to satisfy for it a person possessing infinite merit was required.

10 Q. To satisfy divine justice, was it necessary that Jesus Christ should be both God and man?
A. Yes; to be able to suffer and die it was necessary that Jesus Christ should be man; while for His sufferings to be of infinite value it was necessary that He should be God.

11 Q. Why was it necessary that the merits of Jesus Christ should be of infinite value?
A. It was necessary that the merits of Jesus Christ should be of

infinite value, because God's Majesty, which had been offended by sin, is infinite.

12 Q. Was it necessary for Jesus Christ to suffer as much as He actually did?
A. No, it was not absolutely necessary for Jesus Christ to suffer as much as He did, because each of His acts being of infinite value, the least of His sufferings would have sufficed for our redemption.

13 Q. Why, then, did Jesus suffer so much?
A. Jesus Christ suffered so much in order to satisfy divine justice all the more abundantly; to display His love for us still more; and to inspire us with the deepest horror of sin.

14 Q. Did anything remarkable happen at the death of Jesus Christ?
A. Yes, at the death of Jesus Christ, the sun was darkened the earth trembled, graves opened and many of the dead arose.

15 Q. Where was the Body of Jesus Christ buried?
A. The Body of Jesus Christ was buried in a new grave, hewn out of a rock, on the mount not far from where He had been crucified.

16 Q. Was the Divinity separated from the Body and Soul of Jesus Christ by His death?
A. The Divinity was separated from neither the Body nor the Soul of Christ in death; only the Soul was separated from the Body.

17 Q. For whom did Jesus Christ die?
A. Jesus Christ died for the salvation of all men, and made satisfaction for all.

18 Q. If Jesus Christ died for the salvation of all men, why are not all men saved?
A. Jesus Christ died for all, but not all are saved, because not all

The Apostles Creed

will acknowledge Him; all do not observe His Law; all do not avail themselves of the means of salvation He has left us.

19 Q. To be saved is it enough that Jesus Christ has died for us?
A. No, it is not enough for our salvation that Jesus Christ has died for us; it is also necessary that the fruit of His Passion and death be applied to each one of us, which is accomplished especially by means of the Sacraments instituted for this end by Jesus Christ Himself; and as many either do not receive the Sacraments at all, or do not receive them well, they thus render the death of Jesus Christ useless in their regard.

The Fifth Article of the Creed

1 Q. What are we taught in the Fifth Article: *He descended into hell; the third day He rose again from the dead?*
A. The Fifth Article of the Creed teaches us that the Soul of Jesus Christ, on being separated from His Body, descended to the Limbo of the holy Fathers, and that on the third day it became united once more to His Body, never to be parted from it again.

2 Q. What is here meant by *hell?*
A. Hell here means the *Limbo of the holy Fathers*, that is, the place where the souls of the just were detained, in expectation of redemption through Jesus Christ.

3 Q. Why were not the souls of the Holy Fathers admitted into heaven before the death of Jesus Christ?
A. The souls of the holy Fathers were not admitted into heaven before the death of Jesus Christ, because heaven was closed by the sin of Adam, and it was but fitting that Jesus Christ, who reopened it by His death, should be the first to enter it.

4 Q. Why did Jesus Christ defer His own resurrection until the third day?
A. Jesus Christ deferred His own resurrection until the third day to show clearly that He was really dead.

5 Q. Was the resurrection of Jesus Christ like the resurrection of other men who had been raised from the dead?
A. No, the resurrection of Jesus Christ was not like the resurrection of other men who had been raised from the dead, because He rose by His own power, while the others were raised by the power of God.

The Sixth Article of the Creed

1 Q. What are we taught in the Sixth Article: *He ascended into heaven, sitteth at the right hand of God, the Father Almighty?*
A. The Sixth Article of the Creed teaches us that Jesus Christ, forty days after His resurrection, ascended of Himself into heaven in the sight of His Apostles; and that while as God He was equal to His Father in glory, as man He has been raised above all the Angels and Saints, and constituted Lord of all things.

2 Q. Why did Jesus Christ remain forty days on earth after His resurrection before ascending into heaven?
A. After His resurrection Jesus Christ remained forty days on earth before ascending into heaven, to prove by several apparitions that He was truly risen, to instruct the Apostles still further, and to confirm them in the truths of faith.

3 Q. Why did Jesus Christ ascend into heaven?
A. Jesus Christ ascended into heaven:
    (1) To take possession of the Kingdom He had merited by His death;

The Apostles Creed

    (2) To prepare the place of our glory, and to be our Mediator and Advocate with the Father;

    (3) To send the Holy Ghost upon His Apostles.

4 Q. Why is it said of Jesus Christ that He ascended, and of His Most Holy Mother that she was assumed, into heaven?
A. It is said of Jesus Christ that He ascended into heaven, and of His Most Holy Mother that she was assumed, because, Jesus Christ, being Man-God, ascended into heaven by His own power; but His Mother, being a creature, even though the greatest of all creatures, was taken up into heaven by the power of God.

5 Q. Explain the words: *Sitteth at the right hand of God, the Father Almighty.*
A. The word *sitteth* signifies the peaceful possession which Jesus Christ has of His glory; and the words: *At the right hand of God, the Father Almighty,* denote that He has a place of honour above all creatures.

The Seventh Article of the Creed

1 Q. What are we taught in the Seventh Article: *From thence He shall come to judge the living and the dead?*
A. The Seventh Article of the Creed teaches us that at the end of the world Jesus Christ, in all His glory and majesty, will come from heaven to judge all men, both good and bad, and to give to each of them the reward or the punishment he shall have merited.

2 Q. If every one has to be judged by Jesus Christ in particular judgment immediately after death, why must all be judged in the general judgment?
A. We must all be judged in the general judgment for several reasons:

    (1) That God may be glorified;

(2) That Jesus Christ may be glorified;
(3) That the Saints may be glorified;
(4) That the wicked may be confounded;
(5) That along with the soul the body may receive its sentence of reward or punishment.

3 Q. How will God's glory be manifested in the General Judgment?
A. God's glory will be manifested in the General Judgment in this way, that all shall then know how justly God governs the world, even though here on earth the good are often afflicted and the wicked are often in prosperity.

4 Q. How will the glory of Jesus Christ be manifested in the General Judgment?
A. The glory of Jesus Christ will be manifested in the General Judgment in this way, that He who was unjustly condemned by men, shall then come before the whole world as the Supreme Judge of all.

5 Q. How will the glory of the Saints be manifested in the General Judgment?
A. The glory of the Saints will be manifested in the General Judgment in this way, that many of them who died despised by the wicked, shall be glorified before the whole world.

6 Q. How great will be the confusion of the wicked in the General Judgment?
A. In the General Judgment great indeed shall be the confusion of the wicked, especially of those who have oppressed the just and who have tried in this life to be esteemed as men of virtue and goodness; for they shall then see even their most hidden sins laid bare before the whole world.

The Eighth Article of the Creed

1. Q. What are we taught in the Eighth Article: *I believe in the Holy Ghost?*
A. The Eighth Article of the Creed teaches us that there is a Holy Ghost, the Third Person of the Blessed Trinity; and that, like the Father and the Son, He is God eternal, infinite, omnipotent, Creator and Lord of all things.

2. Q. From whom does the Holy Ghost proceed?
A. The Holy Ghost proceeds from the Father and the Son, as from one Principle, by way of will and love.

3. Q. If the Son proceeds from the Father, and the Holy Ghost proceeds from the Father and the Son, it would seem as if the Father and the Son are prior to the Holy Ghost; how then can it be said that all the Three Persons are eternal?
A. It is said that all the Three Persons are eternal, because the Father has begotten the Son from all eternity, and the Holy Ghost proceeds from the Father and from the Son from all eternity.

4. Q. Why is the Third Person of the Blessed Trinity specially designated by the name of the Holy Ghost or the Holy Spirit?
A. The Third Person of the Blessed Trinity is specially designated by the name of the Holy Ghost or the Holy Spirit, because He proceeds from the Father and from the Son by way of spiration[4] and of love.

---

[4] The word *'spiration'* has been made up from the Latin word *Spiritus*, traditionally used to refer to the Third Person of the Blessed Trinity; the traditional English term is the Holy Ghost. *Spiration* gives the idea of a breathing, or a "sigh of love."

5 Q. What work is especially attributed to the Holy Ghost?
A. To the Holy Ghost is specially attributed the sanctification of souls.

6 Q. Do the Father and the Son sanctify us equally with the Holy Ghost?
A. Yes, all the Three Divine Persons equally sanctify us.

7 Q. If this is so, why is the sanctification of souls specially attributed to the Holy Ghost?
A. The sanctification of souls is specially attributed to the Holy Ghost, because it is a work of love, and the works of love are attributed to the Holy Ghost.

8 Q. When did the Holy Ghost descend on the Apostles?
A. The Holy Ghost descended on the Apostles on the day of Pentecost, that is, fifty days after the Resurrection of Jesus Christ, and ten days after His Ascension.

9 Q. Where were the Apostles during the ten days preceding Pentecost?
A. The Apostles were gathered together in the Supper Room with the Virgin Mary and the other disciples, and were persevering in prayer in expectation of the Holy Ghost, Whom Jesus Christ had promised to send them.

10 Q. What effects did the Holy Ghost produce in the Apostles?
A. The Holy Ghost confirmed the Apostles in the faith, filled them with light, strength, charity, and an abundance of all His gifts.

11 Q. Was the Holy Ghost sent for the Apostles alone?
A. The Holy Ghost was sent for the whole Church and for every faithful soul.

12 Q. What does the Holy Ghost do in the Church?
A. The Holy Ghost gives life to the Church by His grace and by

The Apostles Creed

His gifts, as the soul gives life to the body; He establishes in her the Kingdom of truth and of love; and He helps her to lead her children in safety along the way to heaven.

The Ninth Article of the Creed

The Church in General

1 Q. What does the Ninth article: *The Holy Catholic Church, the Communion of Saints,* teach us?
A. The Ninth Article of the Creed teaches us that Jesus Christ founded a visible society on earth called the Catholic Church, and that all those who belong to this Church are in communion with one another.

2 Q. Why immediately after the article that treats of the Holy Ghost is mention made of the Catholic Church?
A. Immediately after the article that treats of the Holy Ghost mention is made of the Catholic Church to indicate that the Church's holiness comes from the Holy Ghost, who is the Author of all holiness.

3 Q. What does the word Church mean?
A. The word Church means a calling forth or assembly of many.

4 Q. Who has convoked or called us into the Church of Jesus Christ?
A. We have been called into the Church of Jesus Christ by a special grace of God, to the end, that by the light of faith and the observance of the divine law, we may render Him the worship due to Him, and attain eternal life.

5 Q. Where are the members of the Church to be found?
A. The members of the Church are found partly in heaven, forming the Church Triumphant; partly in purgatory, forming

the Church Suffering; partly on earth, forming the Church Militant.

6 Q. Do these various parts of the Church constitute one sole Church?
A. Yes, these various parts of the Church constitute one sole Church and one sole body for they have the same Head, Jesus Christ, the same Spirit animating and uniting them, and the same end, eternal happiness, which some already enjoy and the rest hope for.

7 Q. To which part of the Church does this Ninth Article principally refer?
A. This Ninth Article of the Creed principally refers to the Church Militant, which is the Church we actually belong to.

The Church in Particular

8 Q. What is the Catholic Church?
A. The Catholic Church is the Union or Congregation of all the baptised who, still living on earth, profess the same Faith and the same Law of Jesus Christ, participate in the same Sacraments, and obey their lawful Pastors, particularly the Roman Pontiff.

9 Q. State distinctly what is necessary to be a member of the Church?
A. To be a member of the Church it is necessary to be baptised, to believe and profess the teaching of Jesus Christ, to participate in the same Sacraments, and to acknowledge the Pope and the other lawful pastors of the Church.

10 Q. Who are the lawful pastors of the Church?
A. The lawful pastors of the Church are the Roman Pontiff, that is, the Pope, who is Supreme Pastor, and the Bishops. Other

The Apostles Creed

priests, also, and especially Parish Priests, have a share in the pastoral office, subject to the Bishop and the Pope.

11 Q. Why do you say that the Roman Pontiff is supreme Pastor of the Church?
A. Because Jesus Christ said to St. Peter, the first Pope: "Thou art Peter, and upon this rock I will build My Church, and I will give to thee the keys of the Kingdom of Heaven, and whatsoever thou shalt bind on earth shall be bound also in Heaven, and whatsoever thou shalt loose on earth shall be loosed also in Heaven." And again: "Feed My lambs, feed My sheep."

12 Q. The many societies of persons who are baptised but who do not acknowledge the Roman Pontiff as their Head do not, then, belong to the Church of Jesus Christ?
A. No, those who do not acknowledge the Roman Pontiff as their Head do not belong to the Church of Jesus Christ.

13 Q. How can the Church of Jesus Christ be distinguished from the numerous societies or sects founded by men, and calling themselves Christian?
A. From the numerous societies or sects founded by men and calling themselves Christian, the Church of Jesus Christ is easily distinguished by four marks: She is One, Holy, Catholic and Apostolic.

14 Q. Why is the Church called One?
A. The true Church is called One, because her children of all ages and places are united together in the same faith, in the same worship, in the same law; and in participation of the same Sacraments, under the same visible Head, the Roman Pontiff.

15 Q. Can there not be several Churches?
A. No, there cannot be more than one Church; for as there is but one God, one Faith and one Baptism, there is and can be but one true Church.

16 Q. But are not the faithful of a whole Nation or Diocese also called a Church?
A. The faithful of a whole Nation or Diocese are also called a Church, but they ever remain mere parts of the Universal Church and form but one Church with her.

17 Q. Why is the true Church called Holy?
A. The true church is called Holy because holy is her Invisible Head, Jesus Christ; holy are many of her members; holy are her faith, her laws, her Sacraments; and outside of her there is not and cannot be true holiness.

18 Q. Why is the Church called Catholic?
A. The true Church is called Catholic, or Universal, because she embraces the faithful of all times, of all places, of all ages and conditions; and all peoples are called to belong to her.

19 Q. Why is the Church also called Apostolic?
A. The true Church is also called Apostolic because she goes back without a break to the Apostles; because she believes and teaches all that the Apostles believed and taught; and because she is guided and governed by their lawful successors.

20 Q. And why is the true Church called Roman?
A. The true Church is called Roman, because the four marks of Unity, Sanctity, Catholicity and Apostolicity are found in that Church alone which acknowledges as Head the Bishop of Rome, the Successor of St. Peter.

21 Q. What is the constitution of the Church of Jesus Christ?
A. The Church of Jesus Christ has been constituted as a true and perfect Society; and in her we can distinguish a soul and a body.

22 Q. In what does the Soul of the Church consist?
A. The Soul of the Church consists in her internal and spiritual endowments, that is, faith, hope, charity, the gifts of grace and

The Apostles Creed

of the Holy Ghost, together with all the heavenly treasures which are hers through the merits of our Redeemer, Jesus Christ, and of the Saints.

23 Q. In what does the Body of the Church consist?
A. The Body of the Church consists in her external and visible aspect, that is, in the association of her members, in her worship, in her teaching-power and in her external rule and government.

24 Q. To be saved, is it enough to be any sort of member of the Catholic Church?
A. No, to be saved it is not enough to be any sort of member of the Catholic Church; it is necessary to be a living member.

25 Q. Who are the living members of the Church?
A. The living members of the Church are the just, and the just alone, that is, those who are actually in the grace of God.

26 Q. And who are the dead members?
A. The dead members of the Church are the faithful in mortal sin.

27 Q. Can one be saved outside the Catholic, Apostolic and Roman Church?
A. No, no one can be saved outside the Catholic, Apostolic Roman Church, just as no one could be saved from the flood outside the Ark of Noah, which was a figure of the Church.

28 Q. How, then, were the Patriarchs of old, the Prophets, and the other just men of the Old Testament, saved?
A. The just of the Old Testament were saved in virtue of the faith they had in Christ to come, by means of which they spiritually belonged to the Church.

29 Q. But if a man through no fault of his own is outside the Church, can he be saved?
A. If he is outside the Church through no fault of his, that is, if

he is in good faith, and if he has received Baptism, or at least has the implicit desire of Baptism; and if, moreover, he sincerely seeks the truth and does God's will as best he can such a man is indeed separated from the body of the Church, but is united to the soul of the Church and consequently is on the way of salvation.

30 Q. Suppose that a man is a member of the Catholic Church, but does not put her teaching into practice, will he be saved?
A. He who is a member of the Catholic Church and does not put her teaching into practice is a dead member, and hence will not be saved; for towards the salvation of an adult not only Baptism and faith are required, but, furthermore, works in keeping with faith.

31 Q. Are we obliged to believe all the truths the Church teaches us?
A. Yes, we are obliged to believe all the truths the Church teaches us, and Jesus Christ declares that he who does not believe is already condemned.

32 Q. Are we also obliged to do all that the Church commands?
A. Yes, we are obliged to do all that the Church commands, for Jesus Christ has said to the Pastors of the Church: "He who hears you, hears Me, and he who despises you, despises Me."

33 Q. Can the Church err in what she proposes for our belief?
A. No, the Church cannot err in what she proposes for our belief, since according to the promise of Jesus Christ she is unfailingly assisted by the Holy Ghost.

34 Q. Is the Catholic Church infallible, then?
A. Yes, the Catholic Church is infallible, and hence those who reject her definitions lose the faith and become heretics.

The Apostles Creed

35 Q. Can the Catholic Church be destroyed or perish?
A. No; the Catholic Church may be persecuted, but she can never be destroyed or perish. She will last till the end of the world, because Jesus Christ, as He promised, will be with her till the end of time.

36 Q. Why is the Catholic Church so persecuted?
A. The Catholic Church is so persecuted because even her Divine Founder, Jesus Christ, was thus persecuted, and because she reproves vice, combats the passions, and condemns all acts of injustice and all error.

37 Q. Has a Catholic any other duties towards the Church?
A. Every Catholic ought to have a boundless love for the Church, ought to consider himself infinitely honoured and happy in belonging to her, and ought to labour for her glory and advancement by every means in his power.

The Church Teaching and the Church Taught

38 Q. Is there any distinction between the members of the Church?
A. There is a very notable distinction between the members of the Church; for there are some who rule and some who obey; some who teach and some who are taught.

39 Q. What do you call that part of the Church which teaches?
A. That part of the Church which teaches is called the Teaching Church.

40 Q. What do you call that part of the Church which is taught?
A. That part of the Church which is taught is called the Learning Church, or the Church Taught.

41 Q. Who has set up this distinction in the Church?
A. Jesus Christ Himself has established this distinction in the Church.

42 Q. Are the Church Teaching and the Church Taught, then, two churches?
A. The Church Teaching and the Church Taught are two distinct parts of one and the same Church, just as in the human body the head is distinct from the other members, and yet forms but one body with them.

43 Q. Of whom is the Teaching Church composed?
A. The Teaching Church is composed of all the Bishops, with the Roman Pontiff at their head, be they dispersed throughout the world or assembled together in Council.

44 Q. And the Church Taught, of whom is it composed?
A. The Church Taught is composed of all the faithful.

45 Q. Who, then, are they who possess the teaching power in the Church?
A. The teaching power in the Church is possessed by the Pope and the Bishops, and, dependent on them, by the other sacred ministers.

46 Q. Are we obliged to hear the Teaching Church?
A. Yes, without doubt we are obliged under pain of eternal damnation to hear the Teaching Church; for Jesus Christ has said to the Pastors of His Church, in the persons of the Apostles: "He who hears you, hears Me, and he who despises you, despises Me."

47 Q. Besides her teaching power has the Church any other power?
A. Yes, besides her teaching power the Church has in particular the power of administering sacred things, of making laws and of exacting the observance of them.

The Apostles Creed

48 Q. Does the power possessed by the members of the Hierarchy come from the people?
A. The power possessed by the Hierarchy does not come from the people, and it would be heresy to say it did: it comes solely from God.

49 Q. To whom does the exercise of this power belong?
A. The exercise of this power belongs solely to the Hierarchy, that is, to the Pope and to the Bishops subordinate to him.

The Pope and the Bishops

50 Q. Who is the Pope?
A. The Pope, who is also called the Sovereign Pontiff, or the Roman Pontiff, is the Successor of St. Peter in the See of Rome, the Vicar of Jesus Christ on earth, and the visible Head of the Church.

51 Q. Why is the Roman Pontiff the Successor of St. Peter?
A. The Roman Pontiff is the Successor of St. Peter because St. Peter united in his own person the dignity of Bishop of Rome and that of Head of the Church; by divine disposition he established his Seat at Rome, and there died; hence, whosoever is elected Bishop of Rome is also heir to all his authority.

52 Q. Why is the Roman Pontiff the Vicar of Jesus Christ?
A. The Roman Pontiff is the Vicar of Jesus Christ because He represents Him on earth and acts in His stead in the government of the Church.

53 Q. Why is the Roman Pontiff the Visible Head of the Church?
A. The Roman Pontiff is the Visible Head of the Church because he visibly governs her with the authority of Jesus Christ Himself, who is her invisible Head.

54 Q. What, then, is the dignity of the Pope?
A. The dignity of the Pope is the greatest of all dignities on earth, and gives him supreme and immediate power over all and each of the Pastors and of the faithful.

55 Q. Can the Pope err when teaching the Church?
A. The Pope cannot err, that is, he is infallible, in definitions regarding faith and morals.

56 Q. How is it that the Pope is infallible?
A. The Pope is infallible because of the promise of Jesus Christ, and of the unfailing assistance of the Holy Ghost.

57 Q. When is the Pope infallible?
A. The Pope is infallible when, as Pastor and Teacher of all Christians and in virtue of his supreme Apostolic authority, he defines a doctrine regarding faith or morals to be held by all the Church.

58 Q. What sin would a man commit who should refuse to accept the solemn definitions of the Pope?
A. He who refuses to accept the solemn definitions of the Pope, or who even doubts them, sins against faith; and should he remain obstinate in this unbelief, he would no longer be a Catholic, but a heretic.

59 Q. Why has God granted to the Pope the gift of infallibility?
A. God has granted the Pope the gift of infallibility in order that we all may be sure and certain of the truths which the Church teaches.

60 Q. When was it defined that the Pope is infallible?
A. That the Pope is infallible was defined by the Church in the [First] Vatican Council; and should anyone presume to contradict this definition he would be a heretic and excommunicated.

The Apostles Creed

61 Q. In defining that the Pope is infallible, has the Church put forward a new truth of faith?
A. No, in defining that the Pope is infallible the Church has not put forward a new truth of faith; but to oppose new errors she has simply defined that the infallibility of the Pope, already contained in Sacred Scripture and in Tradition, is a truth revealed by God, and therefore to be believed as a dogma or article of faith.

62 Q. How should every Catholic act towards the Pope?
A. Every Catholic must acknowledge the Pope as Father, Pastor, and Universal Teacher, and be united with him in mind and heart.

63 Q. After the Pope, who are they who by Divine appointment are to be most venerated in the Church?
A. After the Pope, those who by Divine appointment are to be most venerated in the Church are the Bishops.

64 Q. Who are the Bishops?
A. The Bishops are the pastors of the faithful; placed by the Holy Ghost to rule the Church of God in the Sees entrusted to them, in dependence on the Roman Pontiff.

65 Q. What is a Bishop in his own diocese?
A. A Bishop in his own diocese is the lawful Pastor, the Father, the Teacher, the Superior of all the faithful, ecclesiastic and lay belonging to his diocese.

66 Q. Why is the Bishop called the lawful Pastor?
A. The Bishop is called the lawful Pastor because the jurisdiction, or the power which he has to govern the faithful of his diocese, is conferred upon him according to the laws and regulations of the Church.

67 Q. To whom do the Pope and the Bishops succeed?
A. The Pope is the successor of St. Peter, the Prince of the

Apostles; and the Bishops are the Successors of the Apostles, in all that regards the ordinary government of the Church.

68 Q. Must the faithful be in union with their Bishop?
A. Yes, all the faithful, ecclesiastic and lay, should be united heart and soul with their Bishop, who is in favour and communion with the Apostolic See.

69 Q. How should the faithful act towards their own Bishop?
A. Each one of the faithful, both ecclesiastic and lay, should revere, love and honour his own Bishop and render him obedience in all that regards the care of souls and the spiritual government of the diocese.

70 Q. By whom is the Bishop assisted in the care of souls?
A. The Bishop is assisted in the care of souls by priests, and especially by Parish Priests.

71 Q. Who is the Parish Priest?
A. The Parish Priest is a priest deputed to preside over and direct with due dependence on his Bishop a portion of the diocese called a parish.

72 Q. What are the duties of the faithful towards their Parish Priest?
A. The faithful should be united with their Parish Priest, listen to him with docility, and show him respect and submission in all that regards the care of the parish.

The Ninth Article of the Creed

The Communion of Saints

1 Q. What are we taught by these words of the Ninth Article: *The Communion of Saints*?
A. In the words *The Communion of Saints,* the Ninth Article of the Creed teaches us that the Church's spiritual goods, both in-

ternal and external, are common to all her members because of the intimate union that exists between them.

2 Q. **Which are the internal goods that are common in the Church?**
A. The internal goods that are common in the Church are: the graces received through the Sacraments; faith, hope and charity; the infinite merits of Jesus Christ; the superabundant merits of the Blessed Virgin and of the Saints; and the fruit of all the good works done in the same Church.

3 Q. **Which are the external goods that are common in the Church?**
A. The external goods that are common in the Church are: the Sacraments, the Sacrifice of the Mass, public prayers, religious functions, and all the other outward practices that unite the faithful.

4 Q. **Do all the children of the Church share in this communion of goods?**
A. All Christians who are in the grace of God share in the communion of internal goods, while those who are in mortal sin do not participate in these goods.

5 Q. **Why do not those who are in mortal sin participate in these goods?**
A. Because that which unites the faithful with God, and with Jesus Christ as His living members, rendering them capable of performing meritorious works for life eternal, is the grace of God which is the supernatural life of the soul; and hence as those who are in mortal sin are without the grace of God, they are excluded from perfect communion in spiritual goods, nor can they accomplish works meritorious towards life eternal.

6 Q. Do Christians then, who are in mortal sin derive no advantage from the internal and spiritual goods of the Church?
A. Christians who are in mortal sin still continue to derive some advantage from the internal and spiritual goods of the Church, inasmuch as they still preserve the Christian character which is indelible, and the virtue of faith which is the basis of justification. They are aided, too, by the prayers and good works of the faithful towards obtaining the grace of conversion to God.

7 Q. Can those in mortal sin participate in the external goods of the Church?
A. Those in mortal sin can participate in the external goods of the Church, unless indeed they are cut off from the Church by excommunication.

8 Q. Why are the members of this Communion, taken together, called saints?
A. The members of this Communion are called saints because all are called to sanctity and have been sanctified by baptism, and because many of them have really attained perfect sanctity.

9 Q. Does the Communion of Saints extend also to heaven and purgatory?
A. Yes, the Communion of Saints also extends to heaven and purgatory, because charity unites the three Churches—the Triumphant, the Suffering and the Militant; the Saints pray to God both for us and for the souls in purgatory; while we on our part give honour and glory to the Saints, and are able to relieve the suffering souls in purgatory by applying on their behalf indulgences and other good works.

Those Outside the Communion of Saints

10 Q. Who are they who do not belong to the Communion of Saints?
A. Those who are damned do not belong to the Communion of Saints in the other life; and in this life those who belong neither to the body nor to the soul of the Church, that is, those who are in mortal sin, and who are outside the true Church.

11 Q. Who are they who are outside the true Church?
A. Outside the true Church are: Infidels, Jews, heretics, apostates, schismatics, and the excommunicated.

12 Q. Who are infidels?
A. Infidels are those who have not been baptised and do not believe in Jesus Christ, because they either believe in and worship false gods as idolaters do, or though admitting one true God, they do not believe in the Messiah, neither as already come in the Person of Jesus Christ, nor as to come; for instance, Mohammedans and the like.

13 Q. Who are the Jews?
A. The Jews are those who profess the Law of Moses; have not received baptism; and do not believe in Jesus Christ.

14 Q. Who are heretics?
A. Heretics are those of the baptised who obstinately refuse to believe some truth revealed by God and taught as an article of faith by the Catholic Church; for example, the Arians, the Nestorians and the various sects of Protestants.

15 Q. Who are apostates?
A. Apostates are those who abjure, or by some external act, deny the Catholic faith which they previously professed.

16 Q. Who are schismatics?
A. Schismatics are those Christians who, while not explicitly

denying any dogma, yet voluntarily separate themselves from the Church of Jesus Christ, that is, from their lawful pastors.

17 Q. Who are the excommunicated?
A. The excommunicated are those who, because of grievous transgressions, are struck with excommunication by the Pope or their Bishop, and consequently are cut off as unworthy from the body of the Church, which, however, hopes for and desires their conversion.

18 Q. Should excommunication be dreaded?
A. Excommunication should be greatly dreaded, because it is the severest and most terrible punishment the Church can inflict upon her rebellious and obstinate children.

19 Q. Of what goods are the excommunicated deprived?
A. The excommunicated are deprived of public prayers, of the Sacraments, of indulgences and of Christian burial.

20 Q. Can we in any way help the excommunicated?
A. We can in some way help the excommunicated and all others who are outside the true Church, by salutary advice, by prayers and good works, begging God in His mercy to grant them the grace of being converted to the faith and of entering into the Communion of Saints.

The Tenth Article of the Creed

1 Q. What are we taught by the Tenth Article: *The Forgiveness of sins?*
A. The Tenth Article of the Creed teaches us that Jesus Christ has left to His Church the power of forgiving sins.

2 Q. Can the Church forgive every sort of sin?
A. Yes, the Church can forgive all sins, no matter how many or how grave they may be, because Jesus Christ has given her full power to bind and to loose.

3. Q. Who exercises this power of forgiving sins in the Church?
A. Those who exercise the power of forgiving sins in the Church are, first of all, the Pope, who alone possesses this power in all its plenitude; then the bishops, and, dependent upon the bishops, the priests.

4. Q. How does the Church forgive sins?
A. The Church forgives sins through the merits of Jesus Christ by conferring the Sacraments instituted by Him for this purpose; especially the sacraments of baptism and penance.

The Eleventh Article of the Creed

1. Q. What are we taught by the Eleventh Article: *The Resurrection of the body?*
A. The Eleventh Article of the Creed teaches us that all men will rise again, every soul resuming the body it had in this life.

2. Q. How will the resurrection of the dead be accomplished?
A. The resurrection of the dead will be accomplished by the virtue of the Omnipotent God, to whom nothing is impossible.

3. Q. When will the resurrection of the dead take place?
A. The resurrection of the dead shall take place at the end of the world, and shall be followed by the General Judgment.

4. Q. Why does God will the resurrection of the body?
A. God wills the resurrection of the body, in order that the soul, having done good or evil while united with the body, may also be rewarded or punished along with it.

5. Q. Will all rise in the same way?
A. No, there will be a vast difference between the bodies of the elect and the bodies of the damned; because only the bodies of the elect shall have, like the risen Christ, the endowments of glorified bodies.

6   Q. What are the endowments that are to adorn the bodies of the elect?
A. The endowments that shall adorn the bodies of the elect are:
   (1) Impassibility, by which they can never again be subject to evil, nor to any kind of pain, nor to need of food, of rest or the like;
   (2) Brightness, by which they shall shine as the sun and as so many stars;
   (3) Agility, by which they shall be able to pass in a moment and without fatigue from one place to another and from earth to heaven;
   (4) Subtlety, by which without hindrance they shall be able to penetrate any body, as did Jesus Christ when risen from the dead.

7   Q. And the bodies of the damned, what of them?
A. The bodies of the damned shall be destitute of all the endowments of the glorified bodies of the blessed, and shall bear upon them the appalling mark of eternal reprobation.

The Twelfth Article of the Creed

1   Q. What are we taught by the Last Article: *Life Everlasting?*
A. The Last Article of the Creed teaches us that, after the present life there is another life, eternally happy for the elect in heaven, or eternally miserable for the damned in hell.

2   Q. Can we comprehend the bliss of heaven?
A. No, we cannot comprehend the bliss of heaven, because it is beyond the scope of our limited minds, and because the goods of heaven cannot be compared with the goods of this world.

3   Q. In what does the happiness of the elect consist?
A. The happiness of the elect consists in for ever seeing, loving and possessing God, the source of all good.

The Apostles Creed

4 Q. In what does the misery of the damned consist?
A. The misery of the damned consists in being for ever deprived of the vision of God and punished with eternal torments in hell.

5 Q. Are the happiness of heaven and the miseries of hell for the soul alone?
A. The happiness of heaven and the miseries of hell at present affect the soul alone, because at present the soul alone is in heaven or in hell; but after the resurrection of the flesh, man in the fullness of his nature, that is, in body and in soul, will be for ever happy or for ever tormented.

6 Q. Shall the bliss of paradise and the miseries of hell be the same for all men?
A. The bliss of heaven in the case of the blessed, and the miseries of hell in the case of the damned, will be the same in substance and in eternal duration; but in measure, or degree, they will be greater or less according to the extent of each one's merits or demerits.

7 Q. What does the word *Amen* signify at the end of the Creed?
A. The word *Amen* at the end of a prayer signifies so be it; at the end of the Creed it signifies so it is, that is to say, "I believe that all things contained in these twelve Articles are most true, and I am more certain of them than if I had seen them with my eyes."

Prayer

Prayer in General

1 Q. What does this Part of Christian Doctrine treat of?
A. This Part of Christian Doctrine treats of Prayer in general, and of the Our Father in particular.

2 Q. What is prayer?
A. Prayer is an elevation of the mind to God to adore Him, to thank Him, and to ask Him for what we need.

3 Q. How is prayer divided?
A. Prayer is divided into mental and vocal prayer. Mental prayer is that made with the mind alone; and vocal prayer is that expressed in words accompanied by attention of mind and devotion of heart.

4 Q. Can prayer be divided in any other way?
A. Prayer may also be divided into private and public prayer.

5 Q. What is private prayer?
A. Private prayer is that which each one says individually for himself or for others.

6 Q. What is public prayer?
A. Public prayer is that said by the Sacred Ministers in the name of the Church and for the salvation of the faithful. That prayer also which is said in common and publicly by the faithful, in processions, pilgrimages and in God's house, may also be called public prayer.

7 Q. Have we a well-founded hope of obtaining by means of prayer the helps and graces of which we stand in need?
A. The hope of obtaining from God the graces of which we stand in need is founded on the promises of the omnipotent, merciful and all-faithful God, and on the merits of Jesus Christ.

8 Q. In whose name should we ask of God the graces we stand in need of?
A. We should ask of God the graces we stand in need of in the Name of Jesus Christ, as He Himself has taught us and as is done by the Church, which always ends her prayers with these words: Through our Lord Jesus Christ.

9 Q. Why should we beg graces of God in the Name of Jesus Christ?
A. We should beg graces of God in the Name of Jesus Christ because He is our Mediator, and it is through Him alone that we can approach the throne of God.

10 Q. If prayer is so powerful how is it that many times our prayers are not heard?
A. Many times our prayers are not heard, either because we ask things not conducive to our eternal salvation, or because we do not ask properly.

11 Q. Which are the chief things we should ask of God?
A. The chief things we should ask of God are His own glory, our eternal salvation and the means of obtaining it.

12 Q. Is it not also lawful to ask for temporal goods?
A. Yes, it is lawful to ask God for temporal goods, but always with the condition that these be in conformity with His Holy will and not a hindrance to our salvation.

13 Q. If God knows all that is necessary for us, why should we pray?
A. Although God knows all that is necessary for us, He nevertheless wills that we should pray to Him so as to acknowledge Him as the Giver of every good gift, to attest our humble submission to Him, and to merit His favours for ourselves.

Prayer

14 Q. What is the first and best disposition to render our prayers efficacious?
A. The first and best disposition to render our prayers efficacious is to be in the state of grace; or if we are not in that state, to desire to put ourselves in it.

15 Q. What other dispositions are required in order to pray well?
A. To pray well we specially require recollection, humility, confidence, perseverance and resignation.

16 Q. What is meant by praying with recollection?
A. It means remembering that we are speaking to God; and hence we should pray with all respect and devotion, as far as possible avoiding distractions, that is, every thought foreign to our prayers.

17 Q. Do distractions lessen the merit of prayer?
A. Yes, when we ourselves bring them about, or when we do not promptly drive them away; but if we do all we can to be recollected in God, then our distractions do not lessen the merit of our prayer, and may even increase it

18 Q. What is required to pray with recollection?
A. Before prayer we should banish all occasions of distraction, and during prayer we should reflect that we are in the presence of God who sees and hears us.

19 Q. What is meant by praying with humility?
A. It means sincerely acknowledging our own unworthiness, powerlessness and misery, and as well as this observing a respectful posture.

20 Q. What is meant by praying with confidence?
A. It means that we should have a firm hope of being heard, if it is to God's glory and our own true welfare.

21 Q. What is meant by praying with perseverance?
A. It means that we should not grow tired of praying, if God does not at once hear us, but that we should ever continue to pray with increased fervour.

22 Q. What is meant by praying with resignation?
A. It means that we should conform our will to the will of God, even when our prayers are not heard, because He knows better than we do what is necessary for our eternal salvation.

23 Q. Does God always hear prayers when well said?
A. Yes, God always hears prayers when well said; but in the way He knows to be most conducive to our eternal salvation, and not always in the way we wish.

24 Q. What effects does prayer produce in us?
A. Prayer makes us recognise our dependence on God, the Supreme Lord, in all things; it makes us think on heavenly things; it makes us advance in virtue; it obtains for us God's mercy; it strengthens us against temptation; it comforts us in tribulation; it aids us in our needs; and it obtains for us the grace of final perseverance.

25 Q. When should we especially pray?
A. We should especially pray when in danger, in temptation, and at the hour of death; moreover, we should pray often, and it is advisable we should do so morning and night, and when beginning the more important actions of the day.

26 Q. For whom should we pray?
A. We should pray for all; first, for ourselves, then for our relatives, superiors, benefactors, friends and enemies; for the conversion of poor sinners, and of those outside the true Church, and for the Holy Souls in Purgatory.

The Lord's Prayer

The Lord's Prayer in General

1 Q. Which is the most excellent of all vocal prayers?
A. The most excellent of all vocal prayers is that which Jesus Christ taught us, that is to say, the *Our Father*.

2 Q. Why is the *Our Father* the most excellent of all prayers?
A. The *Our Father* is the most excellent of all prayers because Jesus Christ Himself composed it and taught it to us; because it contains clearly and in a few words all we can hope for from God; and because it is the standard and model of all other prayers.

3 Q. Is the *Our Father* also the most efficacious of prayers?
A. Yes, it is also the most efficacious of prayers, because it is the most acceptable to God, since in it we pray in the very words His Divine Son has taught us.

4 Q. Why is the *Our Father* called the Lord's prayer?
A. The *Our Father* is called the Lord's Prayer, precisely because Jesus Christ our Lord has taught it to us with His own lips.

5 Q. How many petitions are there in the *Our Father*?
A. In the *Our Father* there are seven petitions preceded by an introduction.

6 Q. Say the *Our Father*.
   (1) Our Father who art in Heaven:
   (2) Hallowed be Thy Name;
   (3) Thy kingdom come;
   (4) Thy will be done on earth as it is in heaven;
   (5) Give us this day our daily bread;

(6) And forgive us our trespasses, as we forgive those who trespass against us;
(7) And lead us not into temptation;
(8) But deliver us from evil. Amen.

7 Q. When invoking God in the beginning of the Lord's Prayer, why do we call Him *Our Father?*
A. In the beginning of the Lord's Prayer we call God *Our Father,* to foster confidence in His infinite goodness by the remembrance that we are his children.

8 Q. How can we say that we are the children of God?
A. We are the children of God: first, because He has created us in His own image, and preserves and governs us by His providence; and secondly, because by an Act of special benevolence He has adopted us in Baptism as brothers of Jesus Christ and co-heirs with Him to eternal glory.

9 Q. Why do we call God *Our Father* and not *my Father?*
A. We call God *Our Father* and not *my Father*, because we are all His children, and hence we should look on and love one another as brothers and pray for one another.

10 Q. God being in every place, why do we say: *Who art in heaven?*
A. God is in every place; but we say: *Our Father who art in heaven,* to raise our hearts to heaven, where God manifests His glory to His children.

The First Petition

11 Q. What do we ask in the First Petition when we say: *Hallowed be Thy Name?*
A. In the First Petition: *Hallowed be Thy Name,* we ask that God may be known, loved, honoured and served by the whole world and by ourselves in particular.

Prayer

12 Q. What do we intend when we ask that God may be known, loved, honoured and served by the whole world?
A. We intend to beg that infidels may come to the knowledge of the Lord God, that heretics may recognise their errors, that schismatics may return to the unity of the Church, that sinners may repent, and that the just may persevere in well-doing.

13 Q. Why do we first of all ask that the Name of God may be sanctified?
A. We first of all ask that the Name of God may be sanctified, because the glory of God should be nearer our hearts than all other goods and interests.

14 Q. How can we promote the glory of God?
A. We can promote the glory of God by prayer, by good example, and by directing to Him all our thoughts, affections and actions.

The Second Petition

15 Q. What do we mean by the Kingdom of God?
A. By the Kingdom of God we mean a threefold spiritual Kingdom; that is, the reign of God in us, or the reign of grace; the reign of God on earth, or the Holy Catholic Church; and the reign of God in heaven, or Paradise.

16 Q. In the words: *Thy Kingdom come,* what do we ask with regard to grace?
A. With regard to grace we beg that God may reign in us by His sanctifying grace, by which He deigns to dwell within us as a king in his palace; and that He may keep us ever united to Himself by the virtues of faith, hope and charity, through which He reigns over our intellect, our heart and our will.

17 Q. In the words: *Thy Kingdom come,* **what do we ask regarding the Church?**
A. Regarding the Church we ask that she may be spread and propagated ever more and more throughout the world for the salvation of mankind.

18 Q. In the words: *Thy Kingdom come,* **what do we ask regarding Heaven?**
A. Regarding Heaven we beg to be one day admitted into that Paradise for which we were created and where we shall be perfectly happy.

The Third Petition

19 Q. What do we ask in the Third Petition: *Thy will be done on earth as it is in Heaven?*
A. In the Third Petition: *Thy will be done on earth as it is in Heaven,* we beg the grace to do the will of God in all things by obeying His Commandments as promptly as the Angels and Saints obey Him in Heaven; and we also beg the grace to correspond to divine inspirations and to live resigned to the will of God should He send us tribulations.

20 Q. Is it necessary to do the will of God?
A. It is as necessary to do the will of God as it is to work out our salvation, because Jesus Christ has said that they alone who have done the will of His Father shall enter into the Kingdom of Heaven.

21 Q. In what way can we know the will of God?
A. We can know the will of God especially by means of the Church and of the spiritual superiors appointed by God to guide us along the way of salvation; we may also learn His most holy will from the divine inspirations that come to us and from the very surroundings in which the Lord has placed us.

22 Q. Should we always recognise the will of God in adversity as well as in prosperity?
A. Both in prosperity and adversity we should always recognise the will of God, who directs or permits all things for our good.

The Fourth Petition

23 Q. What do we ask in the Fourth Petition: *Give us this day our daily bread?*
A. In the Fourth Petition we beg of God all that is daily necessary for soul and body.

24 Q. What do we ask of God for our soul?
A. For our soul we ask of God the sustenance of our spiritual life, that is, we pray the Lord to give us His grace of which we stand in continual need.

25 Q. How is the life of the soul nourished?
A. The life of the soul is nourished principally by the food of the word of God and by the Most Holy Sacrament of the Altar.

26 Q. What do we ask of God for our body?
A. For the body we ask all that is necessary for the sustainment of our temporal life.

27 Q. Why do we say: *Give us this day our daily bread,* rather than: *Give us bread this day?*
A. We say: *Give us this day our daily bread,* rather than: *Give us bread this day,* to exclude all desire of what is another's; and hence we beg the Lord to help us in acquiring just and lawful gains, so that we may procure our maintenance by our own toil and without theft or fraud.

28 Q. Why do we say: *Give us bread,* and not: *Give me bread?*
A. We say: *Give us,* rather than, *Give me,* to remind us that as everything comes from God, so if He gives us His gifts in abun-

dance, He does it in order that we may share what we do not need with the poor.

29 Q. Why do we add: *Daily?*
A. We add, *Daily*, because we should desire that which is necessary to life, and not an abundance of food and other goods of the earth.

30 Q. What more does *Daily* signify in the Fourth Petition?
A. The word *Daily* signifies that we should not be too solicitous regarding the future, but that we should simply ask what we need at present.

The Fifth Petition

31 Q. What do we ask in the Fifth Petition; *And forgive us our trespasses, as we forgive them that trespass against us?*
A. In the Fifth Petition: *And forgive us our trespasses as we forgive them that trespass against us*, we ask God to pardon us our sins as we pardon those who offend us.

32 Q. Why are our sins called debts?
A. Our sins are called debts, because we must satisfy God's justice for them either in this life or in the next.

33 Q. Can those who do not forgive their neighbour hope that God will pardon them?
A. Those who do not forgive their neighbour have no reason to hope that God will pardon them; especially since they condemn themselves when they ask God to forgive them as they forgive their neighbour.

The Sixth Petition

34 Q. What do we ask in the Sixth Petition: *And lead us not into temptation?*
A. In the Sixth Petition: *And lead us not into temptation,* we ask God to deliver us from temptation either by not allowing us to be tempted, or by giving us grace not to be conquered.

35 Q. What are temptations?
A. Temptations are an incitement to sin that comes from the devil, or from the wicked, or from our own evil passions.

36 Q. Is it a sin to have temptations?
A. No, it is no sin to have temptations; but it is a sin to consent to them, or voluntarily to expose oneself to the danger of consenting to them.

37 Q. Why does God allow us to be tempted?
A. God allows us to be tempted so as to test our fidelity, increase our virtue, and augment our merits.

38 Q. What should we do to avoid temptations?
A. To avoid temptation we should fly dangerous occasions, guard our senses, receive the sacraments frequently, and have recourse to the practice of prayer.

The Seventh Petition

39 Q. What do we ask in the Seventh Petition: *But deliver us from evil?*
A. In the Seventh Petition: *But deliver us from evil,* we ask God to free us from evils, past, present, and future, and particularly from the greatest of all evils which is sin, and from eternal damnation, which is its penalty.

40 Q. Why do we say: *Deliver us from evil* and not: *From evils?*
A. We say : *Deliver us from evil,* and not, *from evils,* because we should not desire to be exempt from all the evils of this life, but only from those which are not good for our souls; and hence we beg liberation from evil in general, that is, from whatever God sees would be bad for us.

41 Q. Is it not lawful to beg liberation from some evil in particular, for example, from sickness?
A. Yes, it is lawful to beg liberation from some evil in particular but always in bowing to the will of God, who may even ordain that particular affliction for the good of our soul.

42 Q. How do the tribulations, which God sends us, help us?
A. Tribulations help us to do penance for our sins, to practise virtue, and above all to imitate Jesus Christ, our Head, to whom it is fitting we should conform ourselves in our sufferings, if we wish to have a share in His glory.

43 Q. What is the meaning of *Amen* at the end of the *Our Father?*
A. *Amen* means: So be it; So I do desire; Thus do I pray the Lord; Thus do I hope.

44 Q. To obtain the graces asked in the *Our Father* is it enough to recite it any way at all?
A. To obtain the graces asked in the *Our Father* we must recite it without haste and with attention; and we must put our heart into it.

45 Q. When should we say the *Our Father?*
A. We should say the *Our Father* every day, because every day we have need of God's help.

Prayer

The Hail Mary

1 Q. What prayer do we usually say after the *Our Father?*
A. After the *Our Father* we say the Angelic Salutation, that is, the *Hail Mary,* through which we have recourse to the Blessed Virgin.

2 Q. Why is the *Hail Mary* called the Angelic Salutation?
A. The *Hail Mary* is called the Angelic Salutation, because it begins with the salutation addressed by the Archangel Gabriel to the Virgin Mary.

3 Q. Whose are the words of the *Hail Mary?*
A. The words of the *Hail Mary* are partly the Archangel Gabriel's, partly St. Elizabeth's, and partly the Church's.

4 Q. Which are the words of the Archangel Gabriel?
A. The words of the Archangel Gabriel are these: *Hail, full of grace, The Lord is with thee; blessed art thou among women.*

5 Q. When was it that the angel said these words to Mary?
A. The angel said these words to Mary when he went to announce to her, on the part of God, the mystery of the Incarnation that was to be wrought in her.

6 Q. What is our object in saluting the Blessed Virgin with the very words of the Archangel?
A. In saluting the Blessed Virgin with the words of the Archangel we congratulate her by recalling to mind the singular privileges and gifts which God has granted her in preference to all other creatures.

7 Q. Which are the words of St. Elizabeth?
A. The words of St. Elizabeth are these: *Blessed art thou among women, and blessed is the fruit of thy womb.*

8 Q. When was it that St. Elizabeth said these words?
A. St. Elizabeth, inspired by God, said these words when, three months before she gave birth to St. John the Baptist, she was visited by the Blessed Virgin, who then bore her Divine Son in her womb.

9 Q. What do we intend by saying these words?
A. In saying the words of St. Elizabeth we congratulate the Blessed Virgin on her high dignity as Mother of God, and we bless God and thank Him for having given us Jesus Christ through Mary.

10 Q. Whose are the other words of the *Hail Mary*?
A. All the other words of the *Hail Mary* have been added by the Church.

11 Q. What do we ask in the last part of the *Hail Mary*?
A. In the last part of the *Hail Mary* we beg the protection of the Blessed Virgin during this life and especially at the hour of death, when we shall have greater need of it.

12 Q. Why do we say the *Hail Mary*, rather than any other prayer, after the *Our Father*?
A. Because the Blessed Virgin is our most powerful advocate with Jesus Christ, and hence, after having said the prayer taught us by Jesus Christ, we pray the Blessed Virgin to obtain for us the graces we have asked therein.

13 Q. Why is the Blessed Virgin so powerful?
A. The Blessed Virgin is so powerful, because, being the Mother of God, she cannot but be heard by Him.

14 Q. What do the Saints teach us on devotion to Mary?
A. Regarding devotion to Mary the Saints teach us that those who are truly devout to her are loved and protected by her with a most tender Mother's love, and that with her help they are sure to find Jesus and obtain Paradise.

15 Q. What form of devotion to Mary does the Church recommend in a very special manner?
A. The devotion to the Blessed Virgin which the Church specially recommends is the Holy Rosary.

The Sacraments

Nature of the Sacraments

1. Q. What is treated of in the fourth part of the Christian Doctrine?
A. In the fourth part of the Christian Doctrine the sacraments are treated of.

2. Q. What is meant by the word *sacrament*?
A. By the word *sacrament* is meant a sensible and efficacious sign of grace, instituted by Christ to sanctify our souls.

3. Q. Why do you call the sacraments sensible and efficacious signs of grace?
A. I call the sacraments sensible and efficacious signs of grace because all the sacraments signify by means of sensible things, the divine grace which they produce in our souls.

4. Q. Show by an example how the sacraments are sensible and efficacious signs of grace.
A. In Baptism the pouring of water on the head of the person, and the words : "I baptise thee," that is, I wash thee, "in the name of the Father, and of the Son, and of the Holy Ghost," are a sensible sign of that which Baptism accomplishes in the soul; just as water washes the body, so in like manner does the grace given in Baptism cleanse the soul from sin.

5. Q. How many sacraments are there, and what are they called?
A. There are seven sacraments: Baptism, Confirmation, Eucharist, Penance, Extreme Unction, Holy Orders and Matrimony.

6 Q. What is necessary to constitute a sacrament?
A. To constitute a sacrament it is necessary to have the matter, the form, and the minister, who must have the intention to do what the Church does.

7 Q. What is the matter of the sacraments?
A. The matter of the sacraments is the sensible thing made use of in effecting the sacrament; such as, for example, natural water in Baptism, oil and balsam in Confirmation.

8 Q. What is the form of the sacraments?
A. The form of the sacraments is the words which are pronounced in order to effect the sacrament.

9 Q. Who is the minister of the sacraments?
A. The minister of the sacraments is the person who administers or confers the sacrament.

The Principal Effect of the Sacraments : Grace

10 Q. What is grace?
A. Grace is an inward and supernatural gift given to us without any merit of our own, but through the merits of Jesus Christ in order to gain eternal life.

11 Q. How is grace distinguished?
A. Grace is divided into sanctifying grace, which is also called habitual grace, and actual grace.

12 Q. What is sanctifying grace?
A. Sanctifying grace is a supernatural gift inherent in our soul, and rendering us just, adopted children of God and heirs to Paradise.

13 Q. How many kinds of sanctifying grace are there?
A. Sanctifying grace is of two kinds: first grace and second grace.

The Sacraments

14 Q. What is first grace?
A. First grace is that by means of which one passes from the state of mortal sin to the state of justice.

15 Q. And what is second grace?
A. Second grace is an increase of first grace.

16 Q. What is actual grace?
A. Actual grace is a supernatural gift which enlightens the mind, moves and strengthens the will in order to enable us to do good and avoid evil.

17 Q. Can we resist the grace of God?
A. Yes, we can resist the grace of God because it does not destroy our free will.

18 Q. By the aid of our own powers alone can we do anything available to life eternal?
A. Without the help of the grace of God, and by our own powers alone, we cannot do anything helpful to life everlasting.

19 Q. How is grace given us by God?
A. Grace is given us by God chiefly through the sacraments.

20 Q. Do the sacraments confer any other grace besides sanctifying grace?
A. Besides sanctifying grace the sacraments also confer sacramental grace.

21 Q. What is sacramental grace?
A. Sacramental grace consists in the right acquired in the reception of a sacrament, to have at the proper time the actual graces necessary to fulfil the obligations arising from the sacrament received. Thus when we were baptised we received the right to have the grace to live a Christian life.

22 Q. Do the sacraments always confer grace on those who receive them?
A. The sacraments always confer grace provided they are received with the necessary dispositions.

23 Q. Who gave to the sacraments the power of conferring grace?
A. Jesus Christ by His passion and death gave to the sacraments the power of conferring grace.

24 Q. What sacraments confer first sanctifying grace?
A. The sacraments which confer first sanctifying grace, and render us friends of God, are two: Baptism and Penance.

25 Q. How are these two sacraments called on that account?
A. These two sacraments, Baptism and Penance, are on that account called sacraments of the dead, because they are instituted chiefly to restore to the life of grace the soul dead by sin.

26 Q. Which are the sacraments that increase grace in those who already possess it?
A. The sacraments which increase grace in those who already possess it are the other five: Confirmation, Eucharist, Extreme Unction, Holy Orders and Matrimony, all of which confer second grace.

27 Q. On this account how are they called?
A. These five sacraments—Confirmation, Eucharist, Extreme Unction, Holy Orders and Matrimony—are on that account called sacraments of the living, because those who receive them must be free from mortal sin, that is, already alive through sanctifying grace.

The Sacraments

28 Q. What sin does he commit who, conscious that he is not in a state of grace, receives one of the sacraments of the living?
A. He who conscious that he is not in a state of grace, receives one of the sacraments of the living, commits a serious sacrilege.

29 Q. What sacraments are most necessary for salvation?
A. The sacraments most necessary to salvation are two: Baptism and Penance. Baptism is necessary to all, and Penance is necessary to all who have sinned mortally after Baptism.

30 Q. What is the greatest of all the sacraments?
A. The greatest of all the sacraments is the Eucharist, because it contains not only grace, but also Jesus Christ the Author of Grace and of the sacraments.

The Character Impressed by some of the Sacraments

31 Q. What sacraments can be received only once?
A. The sacraments that can be received only once are three: Baptism, Confirmation, and Holy Orders.

32 Q. Why can the three sacraments of Baptism, Confirmation and Holy Orders be received only once?
A. The three sacraments, Baptism, Confirmation and Holy Orders can be received only once, because each of them imprints a special character on the soul.

33 Q. What is the character that each of the three sacraments, Baptism, Confirmation and Holy Orders imprints on the soul?
A. The character that each of the three sacraments, Baptism, Confirmation, and Holy Orders imprints on the soul is a spiritual mark that is never effaced.

34 Q. What is the purpose of the character that these three sacraments impress on the soul?
A. The character that these three sacraments imprint on the soul, serves to mark us as members of Jesus Christ at Baptism, as His soldiers at Confirmation, and as His ministers at Holy Orders.

Baptism

Nature and Effects of Baptism

1 Q. What is the sacrament of Baptism?
A. Baptism is a sacrament by which we are born again to the grace of God, and become Christians.

2 Q. What are the effects of the sacrament of Baptism?
A. The sacrament of Baptism confers first sanctifying grace by which original sin is washed away, as well as all actual sin if any such exists; it remits all punishment due on account of such sins; it imprints the character of a Christian; it makes us children of God, members of the Church, and heirs to Paradise, and enables us to receive the other sacraments.

3 Q. What is the matter of Baptism?
A. The matter of Baptism is natural water which is poured on the head of the person to be baptised in such a quantity as to flow.

4 Q. What is the form of Baptism?
A. The form of Baptism is: "I baptise thee in the name of the Father and of the Son and of the Holy Ghost."

The Sacraments

Minister of Baptism

5 Q. To whom does it belong to confer Baptism?
A. To confer Baptism belongs by right to bishops and parish priests, but in case of necessity any person, whether man or woman, even a heretic or an infidel, can administer it, provided he carries out the rite of Baptism, and has the intention of doing what the Church does.

6 Q. If it were necessary to baptise a person in danger of death, and if several people were present, who should administer the sacrament?
A. If it were necessary to baptise a person in danger of death, and if several people were present, a priest, if such were at hand, should administer the Sacrament, and, in his absence, one of the inferior clergy; and in the absence of such, a layman in preference to a woman, unless in the case in which the greater skill on the part of the woman, or the claims of propriety, should demand otherwise.

7 Q. What intention should the person baptising have?
A. The person baptising should have the intention of doing what Holy Church does in baptising.

The Rite of Baptism and the Disposition of the Adult who Receives It

8 Q. How is Baptism given?
A. Baptism is given by pouring water on the head of the person to be baptised—and if it cannot be poured on the head, then on some other principal part of the body—saying at the same time: "I baptise thee in the name of the Father, and of the Son, and of the Holy Ghost."

9 Q. If one were to pour the water and another to pronounce the words would the person be baptised?
A. If one poured the water and another said the words the person would not be baptised; because it is necessary that the person who pours the water should pronounce the words.

10 Q. When in doubt whether the person is dead, is it right to omit baptising him?
A. When in doubt whether the person is dead, he should be baptised conditionally, saying: "If thou art alive I baptise thee in the name of the Father, and of the Son, and of the Holy Ghost."

11 Q. When should infants be brought to the Church to be baptised?
A. Infants should be brought to the Church to be baptised as soon as possible.

12 Q. Why such anxiety to have infants receive Baptism?
A. There should be the greatest anxiety to have infants baptised because, on account of their tender age, they are exposed to many dangers of death, and cannot be saved without Baptism.

13 Q. Do parents sin, then, who, through negligence, allow their children to die without Baptism, or who defer it?
A. Yes, fathers and mothers who, through negligence, allow their children to die without Baptism sin grievously, because they deprive their children of eternal life; and they also sin grievously by putting off Baptism for a long time, because they expose them to danger of dying without having received it.

14 Q. When the person who is being baptised is an adult, what dispositions should he have?
A. An adult who is being baptised, besides faith, should have at least imperfect contrition for the mortal sins he may have committed.

The Sacraments

15 Q. If an adult in mortal sin was baptised without such sorrow, what would he receive?
A. If an adult was baptised in mortal sin without such sorrow he would receive the character of Baptism, but not the remission of his sins nor sanctifying grace. And these two effects would be suspended, until the obstacle is removed by perfect contrition or by the sacrament of Penance.

Necessity of Baptism and Obligations of the Baptised

16 Q. Is Baptism necessary to salvation?
A. Baptism is absolutely necessary to salvation, for our Lord has expressly said: "Unless a man be born again of water and the Holy Ghost, he cannot enter into the Kingdom of God."

17 Q. Can the absence of Baptism be supplied in any other way?
A. The absence of Baptism can be supplied by martyrdom, which is called Baptism of Blood, or by an act of perfect love of God, or of contrition, along with the desire, at least implicit, of Baptism, and this is called Baptism of Desire.

18 Q. To what is the person baptised bound?
A. The person baptised is bound to always profess the faith and observe the Law of Jesus Christ and of His Church.

19 Q. In receiving holy Baptism what do we renounce?
A. In receiving holy Baptism we renounce, for ever, the devil, his works and pomps.

20 Q. What is meant by the works and pomps of the devil?
A. By the works and pomps of the devil we mean sin and the maxims of the world that are contrary to the maxims of the Gospel.

Names and Sponsors

21 Q. Why is the name of a saint given to him who is being baptised?
A. To him who is being baptised is given the name of a saint in order to put him under the protection of a heavenly patron and to animate him to imitate that saint's example.

22 Q. Who are the godfathers and godmothers in Baptism?
A. The godfathers and godmothers in Baptism are those persons who, in accordance with the decree of the Church, hold the infants at the font, answer for them, and become guarantees in the sight of God for their Christian education, especially in the absence of the parents.

23 Q. Are we obliged to keep the promises and renunciations made for us by our sponsors?
A. We are certainly obliged to observe the promises and renunciations made for us by our sponsors, because it is only on this condition that God has received us into His grace.

24 Q. What sort of persons should be chosen as godfathers and godmothers?
A. There should be chosen as godfathers and godmothers Catholics of good life, and obedient to the laws of the Church.

25 Q. What are the obligations of godfathers and godmothers?
A. Godfathers and godmothers are bound to see that their spiritual children are instructed in the truths of faith, and live as good Christians and they should edify them by their good example.

26 Q. What tie do sponsors contract in Baptism?
A. Sponsors contract a spiritual relationship with the baptised and with the parents of the baptised, which causes an impediment to marriage with these persons.

Chrism or Confirmation

1 Q. What is the sacrament of Confirmation?
A. Confirmation is a sacrament which gives us the Holy Ghost, imprints on our souls the mark of a soldier of Jesus Christ, and makes us perfect Christians.

2 Q. How does the sacrament of Confirmation make us perfect Christians?
A. The sacrament of Confirmation makes us perfect Christians by confirming us in the faith and perfecting the other virtues and gifts received in Baptism; hence it is called Confirmation.

3 Q. What gifts of the Holy Ghost are received in Confirmation?
A. The gifts of the Holy Ghost received in Confirmation are these seven: Wisdom, Understanding, Counsel, Fortitude, Knowledge, Piety, and the Fear of the Lord.

4 Q. What is the matter of this sacrament?
A. The matter of this sacrament, besides the imposition of hands by the bishop, is the anointing of the forehead of the baptised with sacred chrism; and for this reason it is also called the sacrament of Chrism, that is Anointing.

5 Q. What is sacred Chrism?
A. Sacred Chrism is oil of olive mingled with balsam, and consecrated by the bishop on Holy Thursday.

6 Q. What do the oil and balsam in this sacrament signify?
A. In this sacrament the oil, which is unctuous and strengthening, signifies the abounding grace which is diffused over the soul of the Christian to confirm him in his faith; and the balsam, which is fragrant and prevents corruption, signifies that the Christian, strengthened by this grace, is enabled to give forth a good odour of Christian virtue and preserve himself from the corruption of vice.

7 Q. What is the form of the sacrament of Confirmation?
A. The form of the sacrament of Confirmation is this: "I sign thee with the Sign of the Cross, and I confirm thee with the chrism of salvation, in the Name of the Father, and of the Son, and of the Holy Ghost. Amen."

8 Q. Who is the minister of the sacrament of Confirmation?
A. The ordinary minister of the sacrament of Confirmation is the bishop alone.

9 Q. How does the bishop administer Confirmation?
A. In administering the sacrament of Confirmation the bishop first stretches his hands over those to be confirmed, and invokes the Holy Ghost upon them; next, he anoints the forehead of each one with sacred chrism in the form of a cross, saying the words of the form; then he gives each one confirmed a light stroke on the cheek with his right hand, saying: Peace be with you; finally, he solemnly blesses all those he has confirmed.

10 Q. Why is the anointing made on the forehead?
A. The anointing is made on the forehead, where signs of fear and shame appear, in order that he who is confirmed may understand that he should not blush at the name and profession of a Christian, nor fear the enemies of his faith.

11 Q. Why is a light stroke given to the person confirmed?
A. A light stroke is given to the person confirmed to show him that he should be ready to bear all insults and endure all sufferings for the faith of Jesus Christ.

12 Q. Should all endeavour to receive the sacrament of Confirmation?
A. Yes, all should endeavour to receive the sacrament of Confirmation and to have those under them receive it.

The Sacraments

13 Q. At what age is it advisable to receive the sacrament of Confirmation?
A. The age at which it is advisable to receive the sacrament of Confirmation is about the seventh year, because it is then that temptations usually begin, and the grace of the sacrament can be sufficiently discerned and a recollection be had of having received it.[5]

14 Q. What dispositions are required to receive worthily the sacrament of Confirmation?
A. To receive worthily the sacrament of Confirmation it is necessary to be in the grace of God; know the principal mysteries of our holy faith; and approach it with reverence and devotion.

15 Q. Would he who received Confirmation a second time be guilty of sin?
A. He would commit a sacrilege; because Confirmation is one of the sacraments that imprint a character on the soul and hence may be received only once.

16 Q. What should a Christian do to preserve the grace of Confirmation?
A. To preserve the grace of Confirmation a Christian should pray often, do good works, and live according to the laws of Jesus Christ, in spite of human respect.

17 Q. Why are there also godfathers and godmothers in Confirmation?
A. In order that, by word and example, they may show the confirmed the way to eternal life and help him in the spiritual combat.

---

[5] The Catechism of the Council of Trent says: "It is not expedient to administer it to children who have not yet attained the use of reason. Hence if it does not seem well to defer it to the twelfth year, it is highly proper to defer it at least to the seventh year." The current practice is around ninth or tenth year, or two years after first Communion.

18 Q. What qualifications are required in sponsors?
A. They should be of proper age, Catholics, confirmed, instructed in the necessary truths of religion, and persons of good life.

19 Q. Does a sponsor in Confirmation contract any relationship with the confirmed and the parents of the confirmed?
A. The sponsor in Confirmation contracts the same spiritual relationship as is contracted in Baptism.

The Blessed Eucharist

The Nature of This Sacrament—The Real Presence

1 Q. What is the sacrament of the Eucharist?
A. The Eucharist is a sacrament in which, by the marvellous conversion of the whole substance of bread into the Body of Jesus Christ, and that of wine into His precious Blood, is contained truly, really, and substantially, the Body, the Blood, the Soul and Divinity of the same Lord Jesus Christ, under the appearance of bread and wine as our spiritual food.

2 Q. In the Eucharist is there the same Jesus Christ who is in heaven, and who was born on earth of the Blessed Virgin?
A. Yes, in the Eucharist there is truly the same Jesus Christ who is in heaven, and who was born on earth of the Blessed Virgin.

3 Q. Why do you believe that in the Eucharist Jesus Christ is really present?
A. I believe that in the Eucharist Jesus Christ is truly present, because He Himself has said it, and holy Church teaches it.

The Sacraments

4 Q. What is the matter of the sacrament of the Eucharist?
A. The matter of the sacrament of the Eucharist is that which was used by Jesus Christ Himself, that is, wheaten bread and wine of the vine.

5 Q. What is the form of the sacrament of the Eucharist?
A. The form of the sacrament of the Eucharist consists of the words used by Jesus Christ Himself: "This is My Body: This is My Blood."

6 Q. What is the host before consecration?
A. The host before consecration is bread.

7 Q. After consecration what is the host?
A. After consecration the host is the true Body of our Lord Jesus Christ under the species of bread.

8 Q. What is in the chalice before consecration?
A. In the chalice before consecration there is wine with a few drops of water.

9 Q. After consecration what is in the chalice?
A. After consecration there is in the chalice the true Blood of our Lord Jesus Christ, under the species of wine.

10 Q. When does the change of the bread into the Body and of the wine into the Blood of Jesus Christ take place?
A. The change of the bread into the Body and of the wine into the Blood of Jesus Christ is made in the very moment in which the priest pronounces the words of consecration during holy Mass.

11 Q. What is the consecration?
A. The consecration is the renewal, by means of the priest, of the miracle wrought by Jesus Christ at the Last Supper, of changing bread and wine into His adorable Body and Blood by saying: "This is My Body: This is My Blood."

12 Q. What does the Church call the miraculous change of bread and of wine into the Body and Blood of Jesus Christ?
A. The Church calls the miraculous change which is daily wrought upon our altars transubstantiation.

13 Q. Who gave this great power to the words of consecration?
A. Our Lord Jesus Christ Himself, who is Almighty God, gave this great power to the words of consecration.

14 Q. Is there nothing left of the bread and of the wine after consecration?
A. After consecration the species of the bread and of the wine alone are left.

15 Q. What are the species of the bread and of the wine?
A. The species of the bread and of the wine are the quantity and sensible qualities of the bread and of the wine, such as the form, the colour, and the taste.

16 Q. How can the species of the bread and of the wine remain without their substance?
A. The species of the bread and of the wine remain without their substance in a wonderful way by the power of God Almighty.

17 Q. Under the species of the bread is there only the Body of Jesus Christ and under the species of the wine only His Blood?
A. Both under the species of the bread and under the species of the wine the living Jesus Christ is all present, with His Body, His Blood, His Soul and His Divinity.

18 Q. Can you tell me why Jesus Christ is whole and entire both in the host and in the chalice?
A. Both in the host and in the chalice Jesus Christ is whole and entire, because He is living and immortal in the Eucharist as He

The Sacraments

is in heaven; hence where His Body is, there also are His Blood, His Soul, and His Divinity; and where His Blood is, there also are His Body, His Soul and His Divinity, all these being inseparable in Jesus Christ.

19 Q. When Jesus Christ is in the host does He cease to be in heaven?
A. When Jesus Christ is in the host He does not cease to be in heaven, but is at one and the same time in heaven and in the Blessed Sacrament.

20 Q. Is Jesus Christ present in all the consecrated hosts in the world?
A. Yes, Jesus Christ is present in all consecrated hosts in the world.

21 Q. How can Jesus Christ be present in all the consecrated hosts in the world?
A. Jesus Christ is present in all the consecrated hosts in the world by the Omnipotence of God, to whom nothing is impossible.

22 Q. When the host is broken is the Body of Jesus Christ broken also?
A. When the host is broken, the Body of Jesus Christ is not broken, but only the species of the bread are broken.

23 Q. In which part of the host is the Body of Jesus Christ?
A. The Body of Jesus Christ is entire in all the parts into which the host is broken.

24 Q. Is Jesus Christ just as much in a particle of a host as in a whole host?
A. Yes, the same Jesus Christ is just as much in a particle of a host as in a whole host.

25 Q. Why is the Most Blessed Eucharist preserved in our churches?
A. The Most Blessed Eucharist is preserved in our churches that It may be adored by the faithful, and brought to the sick when necessary.

26 Q. Ought the Eucharist to be adored?
A. The Eucharist ought to be adored by all, because it contains really, truly, and substantially, our Lord Jesus Christ Himself.

The Institution and Effects of the Sacrament of the Eucharist

27 Q. When did Jesus Christ institute the sacrament of the Eucharist?
A. Jesus Christ instituted the sacrament of the Eucharist at the last supper, which He took with His disciples, the evening before His passion.

28 Q. Why did Jesus Christ institute the Most Holy Eucharist?
A. Jesus Christ instituted the Most Holy Eucharist for three principal reasons:
    (1) To be the Sacrifice of the New Law;
    (2) To be the food of our souls;
    (3) To be a perpetual memorial of His passion and death and a precious pledge both of His love for us and of eternal life.

29 Q. Why did Jesus Christ institute this sacrament under the appearances of bread and wine?
A. Jesus Christ instituted this sacrament under the appearances of bread and wine, because, the Eucharist being intended to be our spiritual nourishment, it was therefore fitting that it should be given to us under the form of food and drink.

The Sacraments

30 Q. What are the effects which the Most Holy Eucharist produces in us?
A. The principal effects which the Most Holy Eucharist produces in those who worthily receive it are these:
  (1) It preserves and increases the life of the soul, which is grace, just as natural food sustains and increases the life of the body;
  (2) It remits venial sins and preserves us from mortal sin;
  (3) It produces spiritual consolation.

31 Q. Does not the Most Holy Eucharist produce other effects in us?
A. Yes; the Most Holy Eucharist produces three other effects in us:
  (1) It weakens our passions, and in particular it allays in us the fires of concupiscence;
  (2) It increases in us the fervour of charity towards God and our neighbour, and aids us to act in conformity with the will of Jesus Christ;
  (3) It gives us a pledge of future glory and of the resurrection of our body.

The Dispositions necessary to Receive Holy Communion worthily

32 Q. Does the sacrament of the Eucharist always produce its marvellous effects in us?
A. The dispositions.

33 Q. What conditions are necessary to make a good Communion?
A. To make a good communion three conditions are necessary:

  (1) To be in the grace of God;

(2) To be fasting from midnight until the moment of Holy Communion;[6]

(3) To know what we are about to receive, and to approach Holy Communion devoutly.

34 Q. What is meant by being in the grace of God?
A. To be in the grace of God means to have a pure conscience and to be free from every mortal sin.

35 Q. What should one who knows that he is in mortal sin do before receiving Communion?
A. One who knows that he is in mortal sin must make a good confession before going to Holy Communion, for even an act of perfect contrition is not enough without confession to enable one who is in mortal sin to receive Holy Communion properly.

36 Q. Why does not even an act of perfect contrition suffice to enable one who knows he is in mortal sin to go to Communion?
A. Because the Church, out of respect for this sacrament, has ordained that no one in mortal sin should dare to go to Communion without first going to confession.

37 Q. Does he who goes to Communion in mortal sin receive Jesus Christ?
A. He who goes to Communion in mortal sin receives Jesus Christ but not His grace; moreover, he commits a sacrilege and renders himself deserving of sentence of damnation.

---

[6] The fast from midnight was the old Eucharistic discipline. In view of evening Masses which became more frequent at his time, Pope Pius XII gave permission to reduce the fast to three hours for solid food and alcoholic drink, and to one hour for non-alcoholic drink (*Christus Dominus*, 6 Jan. 1953). Later, Pope Paul VI reduced the fast to one hour for everything (see 1983 Code #919). This last regulation practically reduces fasting to nothing! Thus the faithful are encouraged to follow the old rules of fast for morning Masses, and Pope Pius XII's regulations for later Masses, keeping the spirit of the Church as Pope Pius XII wrote: "We intend by this Apostolic Letter to confirm the full force of the law and custom concerning the Eucharistic fast; and We also wish to remind those who are able to comply with that law, that they diligently continue to do so, so that only those who need these concessions may make use of them, according to their need." (Ibid.)

The Sacraments

38 Q. What sort of fast is required before Communion?
A. Before ommunion there is required a natural fast which is broken by taking the least thing by way of food or drink.

39 Q. If one were to swallow a particle that had remained between the teeth, or a drop of water while washing, might he still go to Communion?
A. If one were to swallow a particle that had remained between the teeth, or a drop of water while washing, he might still go to Communion, because in both cases these things would either not be taken as food or drink, or they would have already lost the nature of either.

40 Q. Is it ever allowed to go to Communion after having broken the fast?
A. To go to Communion after having broken the fast is permitted to the sick, who are in danger of death, and to those who on account of prolonged illness have received a special dispensation from the Pope. Communion given to the sick in danger of death is called viaticum, because it supports them on their way from this life to eternity.

41 Q. What is meant by the words: *To know what we are about to receive*?
A. *To know what we are about to receive* means to know and firmly believe what is taught in Christian doctrine concerning this sacrament.

42 Q. What do the words: *To receive Holy Communion with devotion* mean?
A. *To receive Holy Communion with devotion* means to approach Holy Communion with humility and modesty in person and dress; and to make a preparation before, and an act of thanksgiving after, Holy Communion.

43 Q. In what does the preparation before Communion consist?
A. Preparation before Communion consists in meditating for some time on Whom we are about to receive, and on who we are; and in making acts of faith, hope, charity, contrition, adoration, humility, and desire to receive Jesus Christ.

44 Q. In what does the thanksgiving after Communion consist?
A. Thanksgiving after Communion consists in keeping ourselves recollected in order to honour the Lord who is within us; renewing our acts of faith, of hope, of charity, of adoration, of thanksgiving, of offerings, and of requests, especially for those graces which are most necessary for ourselves and for those for whom we are bound to pray.

45 Q. What should we do during the day on which we have received Communion?
A. During the day on which we have received Communion, we should remain as recollected as possible, occupy ourselves in works of piety, and discharge the duties of our state with greater diligence.

46 Q. How long does Jesus Christ abide within us after Holy Communion?
A. After Holy Communion Jesus Christ abides within us by His grace as long as we commit no mortal sin; and He abides within us by His Real Presence until the sacramental species are consumed.

The Way to Go to Communion

47 Q. How should we act while receiving Holy Communion?
A. In the act of receiving Holy Communion we should be kneeling, hold our head slightly raised, our eyes modest and

The Sacraments

fixed on the sacred Host, our mouth sufficiently open, and the tongue slightly out over the lips.

48 Q. How should the Communion cloth be held?
A. The Communion cloth should be held in such a way as to receive the sacred Host in case it should fall.

49 Q. When should the sacred Host be swallowed?
A. We should try to swallow the sacred Host as soon as possible, and we should avoid spitting for some time.

50 Q. If the sacred Host should cling to the palate what should be done?
A. If the sacred Host should cling to the palate it should be removed with the tongue, but never with the finger.

The Precept of Holy Communion

51 Q. When are we bound to receive Communion?
A. We are bound to go to Communion once a year, at Easter, each one in his own parish; and also when in danger of death.

52 Q. At what age does the precept of paschal Communion begin to bind?
A. The precept of paschal Communion begins to bind as soon as a child is capable of receiving with the requisite dispositions.

53 Q. Do they sin who are old enough to receive Communion and do not?
A. They who are old enough to receive Communion and do not either because they are unwilling, or because, through their own fault, they are not instructed, undoubtedly sin. Their parents or guardians also sin if the delay of Communion is owing to their fault, and they shall have to render a strict account to God for it.

54 Q. Is it a good and useful thing to go often to Communion?
A. It is an excellent thing to go to Communion often, and even daily in accordance with the desire of the Church, provided we do so with the requisite dispositions.

55 Q. How often may we go to Holy Communion?
A. We may go to Holy Communion as often as we are advised to do so by a pious and learned confessor.

The Holy Sacrifice of the Mass

The Essence, Institution and Ends of the Holy Sacrifice of the Mass

1 Q. Should the Holy Eucharist be considered only as a sacrament?
A. The Holy Eucharist, besides being a sacrament, is also the permanent Sacrifice of the New Law, which Jesus Christ left to His Church to be offered to God by the hands of His priests.

2 Q. In what in general does a sacrifice consist?
A. In general a sacrifice consists in the offering of some sensible thing to God and in some way destroying it as an acknowledgment of His Supreme Dominion over us and over all things.

3 Q. What is this Sacrifice of the New Law called?
A. This Sacrifice of the New Law is called the Holy Mass.

4 Q. What, then, is the Holy Mass?
A. The Holy Mass is the Sacrifice of the Body and Blood of Jesus Christ offered on our altars under the appearances of bread and wine, in commemoration of the Sacrifice of the Cross.

The Sacraments

5 Q. Is the Sacrifice of the Mass the same as that of the Cross?
A. The Sacrifice of the Mass is substantially the same as that of the Cross, for the same Jesus Christ, Who offered Himself on the Cross, it is Who offers Himself by the hands of the priests, His ministers, on our altars; but as regards the way in which He is offered, the Sacrifice of the Mass differs from the Sacrifice of the Cross, though retaining the most intimate and essential relation to it.

6 Q. What difference and relation then is there between the Sacrifice of the Mass and that of the Cross?
A. Between the Sacrifice of the Mass and that of the Cross there is this difference and relation, that on the Cross Jesus Christ offered Himself by shedding His Blood and meriting for us; whereas on our altars He sacrifices Himself without the shedding of His Blood, and applies to us the fruits of His passion and death.

7 Q. What other relation has the Sacrifice of the Mass to that of the Cross?
A. Another relation of the Sacrifice of the Mass to that of the Cross is, that the Sacrifice of the Mass represents in a sensible way the shedding of the Blood of Jesus Christ on the Cross, because, in virtue of the words of consecration, only the Body of our Saviour is made present under the species of the bread and only His Blood under the species of the wine; although by natural concomitance and by the hypostatic union, the living and real Jesus Christ is present under each of the species.

8 Q. Is not the Sacrifice of the Cross the one only Sacrifice of the New Law?
A. The Sacrifice of the Cross is the one only Sacrifice of the New Law, inasmuch as through it Our Lord satisfied Divine Justice, acquired all the merits necessary to save us, and thus, on His part, fully accomplished our redemption. These merits,

however, He applies to us through the means instituted by Him in His Church, among which is the Holy Sacrifice of the Mass.

9 Q. For what ends then is the Holy Sacrifice of the Mass offered?
A. The Sacrifice of the Mass is offered to God for four ends:
   (1) To honour Him properly, and hence it is called Latreutical;
   (2) To thank Him for His favours, and hence it is called Eucharistical;
   (3) To appease Him, make Him due satisfaction for our sins, and to help the souls in Purgatory, and hence it is called Propitiatory;
   (4) To obtain all the graces necessary for us, and hence it is called Impetratory.

10 Q. Who is it that offers to God the Sacrifice of the Holy Mass?
A. The first and principal Offeror of the Sacrifice of the Holy Mass is Jesus Christ, while the priest is the minister who in the Name of Jesus Christ offers the same Sacrifice to the Eternal Father.

11 Q. Who instituted the Sacrifice of the Holy Mass?
A. Jesus Christ Himself instituted the Sacrifice of the Holy Mass when He instituted the Sacrament of the Blessed Eucharist and said that this should be done in memory of His passion.

12 Q. To whom is the Holy Mass offered?
A. The Holy Mass is offered to God alone.

The Sacraments

13 Q. If the Holy Mass is offered to God alone why are so many Masses celebrated in honour of the Blessed Virgin and the Saints?
A. Mass celebrated in honour of the Blessed Virgin and the Saints is always a sacrifice offered to God alone; it is said to be celebrated in honour of the Blessed Virgin and the Saints to thank God for the gifts He has given them, and through their intercession to obtain from Him more abundantly the graces of which we have need.

14 Q. Who shares in the fruits of the Mass?
A. The entire Church shares in the fruits of the Mass, but more particularly:
   (1) The priest and those who assist at Mass, the latter being united with the priest;
   (2) Those for whom the Mass is applied, both living and dead.

The Way to Assist at Mass

15 Q. What is required in order to assist at Holy Mass well and profitably?
A. To assist at Holy Mass well and profitably two things are necessary:
   (1) Modesty of person and
   (2) Devotion of heart.

16 Q. In what does modesty of person consist?
A. Modesty of person consists especially in being modestly dressed, in observing silence and recollection and, as far as possible, in remaining kneeling, except during the time of the two Gospels which are heard standing.

17 Q. In hearing Holy Mass which is the best way to practise true devotion?
A. In hearing Holy Mass the best way to practise true devotion is the following:
   (1) From the very beginning to unite our intention with that of the priest, offering the Holy Sacrifice to God for the ends for which it was instituted.
   (2) To accompany the priest in each prayer and action of the Sacrifice.
   (3) To meditate on the passion and death of Jesus Christ and to heartily detest our sins, which have been the cause of them.
   (4) To go to Communion, or at least to make a spiritual Communion while the priest communicates.

18 Q. What is spiritual Communion?
A. Spiritual Communion is a great desire to be united sacramentally with Jesus Christ. saying, for example: "My Lord Jesus Christ, I desire with my whole heart to be united with Thee now and forever;" and then make the same acts that are to be made before and after sacramental Communion.

19 Q. Does the recitation of the Rosary or other prayers during Mass prevent us from hearing it with profit?
A. The recitation of the Rosary and other prayers during Mass does not prevent us from hearing it with profit, provided we try as far as possible to follow the parts of the Holy Sacrifice.

20 Q. Is it advisable to pray for others while assisting at Mass?
A. Yes it is advisable to pray for others while assisting at Mass; nay more, the time of Holy Mass is the most suitable of all times to pray for the living and the dead.

The Sacraments

21 Q. What should we do after Mass?
A. After Mass we should give God thanks for having allowed us to assist at this great Sacrifice, and we should ask pardon for all the faults we may have committed while assisting at it.

The Sacrament of Penance

Penance in General

1 Q. What is the sacrament of Penance?
A. The sacrament of Penance, also called Confession, is a sacrament instituted by Jesus Christ to remit the sins committed after Baptism.

2 Q. Why is the name of Penance given to this sacrament?
A. The name of Penance is given to this sacrament, because to obtain pardon for sins it is necessary to detest them penitently; and because he who has committed a fault must submit to the penance which the priest imposes.

3 Q. Why is this sacrament also called Confession?
A. This sacrament is also called Confession, because to obtain pardon for sins it is not enough to detest them, but it is necessary also to accuse oneself of them to the priest, that is, to make a confession of them.

4 Q. When did Jesus Christ institute the sacrament of Penance?
A. Jesus Christ instituted the sacrament of Penance on the day of His resurrection when, entering the Supper Room, He solemnly gave His Apostles the power of remitting sin.

5 Q. How did Jesus Christ give His Apostles the power of remitting sin?
A. Jesus Christ gave His Apostles the power of remitting sin thus: Breathing upon them He said: "Receive ye the Holy

Ghost; whose sins you shall forgive they are forgiven; and whose sins you shall retain they are retained."

6 Q. What is the matter of the sacrament of Penance?
A. The matter of the sacrament of Penance is divided into remote and proximate. The remote matter consists of the sins committed by the penitent after Baptism; and the proximate matter are the acts of the penitent himself, that is, contrition, confession and satisfaction.

7 Q. What is the form of the sacrament of Penance?
A. The form of the sacrament of Penance is this: "I absolve thee from thy sins."

8 Q. Who is the minister of the sacrament of Penance?
A. The minister of the sacrament of Penance is a priest authorised by the Bishop to hear confessions.

9 Q. Why do you say that a priest must be authorised by the Bishop?
A. A priest must be authorised by the Bishop to hear confessions because to administer this sacrament validly the power of Orders is not enough, but there is also necessary the power of jurisdiction, that is, the power to judge, which must be given by the Bishop.

10 Q. Which are the parts of the sacrament of Penance?
A. The parts of the sacrament of Penance are contrition, confession, and satisfaction on the part of the penitent, and absolution on the part of the priest.

11 Q. What is contrition or sorrow for sins?
A. Contrition or sorrow for sin is a grief of the soul leading us to detest sins committed and to resolve not to commit them any more.

The Sacraments

12 Q. What does the word contrition mean?
A. Contrition means a crushing or breaking up into pieces as when a stone is hammered and reduced to dust.

13 Q. Why is the name of contrition given to sorrow for sin?
A. The name of contrition is given to sorrow for sin to signify that the hard heart of the sinner is in a certain way crushed by sorrow for having offended God.

14 Q. In what does confession of sins consist?
A. Confession of sins consists in a distinct accusation of our sins made to the confessor in order to obtain absolution and receive penance for them.

15 Q. Why is confession called an accusation?
A. Confession is called an accusation, because it must not be a careless recital, but a true and sorrowful manifestation of our sins.

16 Q. What is satisfaction or penance?
A. Satisfaction or penance is that prayer or other good work which the confessor enjoins on the penitent in expiation of his sins.

17 Q. What is absolution?
A. Absolution is the sentence which the priest pronounces in the name of Jesus Christ when remitting the penitent's sins.

18 Q. Of all the parts of the sacrament of Penance which is the most necessary?
A. Of all the parts of the sacrament of Penance the most necessary is contrition, because without it no pardon for sins is obtainable, while with it alone, perfect pardon can be obtained, provided that along with it there is the desire, at least implicit, of going to confession.

The Effects and the Necessity of the Sacrament of Penance and the Dispositions to Receive It Properly

19 Q. Which are the effects of the sacrament of Penance?
A. The sacrament of Penance confers sanctifying grace by which are remitted the mortal sins and also the venial sins which we confess and for which we are sorry; it changes eternal punishment into temporal punishment, of which it even remits more or less according to our dispositions; it revives the merits of the good works done before committing mortal sin; it gives the soul aid in due time against falling into sin again, and it restores peace of conscience.

20 Q. Is the sacrament of Penance necessary to all for salvation?
A. The sacrament of Penance is necessary for salvation to all who have committed a mortal sin after Baptism.

21 Q. Is it a good thing to go to confession often?
A. Yes, it is an excellent thing to go to confession often, because the sacrament of Penance, besides taking away sin, gives the graces necessary to avoid sin in the future.

22 Q. Has the sacrament of Penance the power of remitting all sins, no matter how numerous or how great they are?
A. The sacrament of Penance has the power of remitting all sins no matter how numerous and great they are, provided it is received with the requisite dispositions.

23 Q. How many conditions are necessary to make a good confession?
A. To make a good confession five things are necessary:
    (1) Examination of conscience;
    (2) Sorrow for having offended God;
    (3) A resolution of sinning no more;
    (4) Confession of our sins;

The Sacraments

  (5) Satisfaction or penance.

24 Q. What should we do first of all to make a good confession?
A. To make a good confession we should first of all earnestly beseech God to give us light to know all our sins and strength to detest them.

Examination of Conscience

25 Q. What is the examination of conscience?
A. The examination of conscience is a diligent search for the sins committed since the last good confession.

26 Q. How is the examination of conscience made?
A. The examination of conscience is made by carefully calling to mind before God all the sins committed but not confessed, in thought, word, deed and omission, against the Commandments of God and the Church, and against the duties of our state.

27 Q. On what else should we examine ourselves?
A. We should also examine ourselves on our bad habits and on the occasions of sin.

28 Q. In our examination should we also try to discover the number of our sins?
A. In our examination we should also try to discover the number of our mortal sins.

29 Q. What is required for a sin to be mortal?
A. For a sin to be mortal three things are required:
  (1) Grave matter,
  (2) Full advertence,
  (3) Perfect consent of the will.

30 Q. When is the matter to be considered grave?
A. The matter is grave when the thing under examination is seriously contrary to the laws of God and His Church.

31 Q. When is there full advertence in sinning?
A. Full advertence in sinning is had when we know perfectly well that we are doing a serious evil.

32 Q. When is perfect consent of the will verified in sinning?
A. Perfect consent of the will is verified in sinning when we deliberately determine to do a thing although we know that thing to be sinful.

33 Q. What diligence should be used in the examination of conscience?
A. In the examination of conscience the same diligence is demanded as is used in a matter of great importance.

34 Q. How much time should be spent in the examination of conscience?
A. More or less time should be spent in the examination of conscience according to the needs of each case, that is, according to the number or kind of sins that burden the conscience and according to the time that has elapsed since the last good confession.

35 Q. How may the examination of conscience be rendered easy?
A. The examination of conscience is rendered easy by making an examination of conscience every evening upon the actions of the day.

Sorrow

36 Q. What is sorrow for sin?
A. Sorrow for sin consists in grief of soul and in a sincere detestation of the offence offered to God.

The Sacraments

37 Q. How many kinds of sorrow are there?
A. Sorrow is of two kinds: perfect sorrow or *contrition;* and imperfect sorrow or *attrition.*

38 Q. What is perfect sorrow or *contrition*?
A. Perfect sorrow is a grief of soul for having offended God because He is infinitely good and worthy of being loved for His own sake.

39 Q. Why do you call the sorrow of contrition perfect sorrow?
A. I call the sorrow of contrition perfect sorrow for two reasons:
   (1) Because it considers the goodness of God alone and not our own advantage or loss;
   (2) Because it enables us at once to obtain pardon for sins, even though the obligation to confess them still remains.

40 Q. Perfect sorrow, then, obtains us pardon of our sins independently of confession?
A. Perfect sorrow does not obtain us pardon of our sins independently of confession, because it always includes the intention to confess them.

41 Q. Why does perfect sorrow or contrition produce the effect of restoring us to the grace of God?
A. Perfect sorrow or contrition produces this effect, because it proceeds from charity which cannot exist in the soul together with sin.

42 Q. What is imperfect sorrow or *attrition*?
A. Imperfect sorrow or *attrition* is that by which we repent of having offended God because He is our Supreme Judge, that is, for fear of the chastisement deserved in this life or in the life to come, or because of the very foulness of sin itself.

43 Q. What qualities must sorrow have to be true sorrow?
A. Sorrow in order to be true must have four qualities: It must be internal, supernatural, supreme and universal.

44 Q. What is meant by saying that sorrow must be internal?
A. It means that it must exist in the heart and will, and not in words alone.

45 Q. Why must sorrow be internal?
A. Sorrow must be internal because the will, which has been alienated from God by sin, must return to God by detesting the sin committed.

46 Q. What is meant by saying that sorrow must be supernatural?
A. It means that it must be excited in us by the grace of God and conceived through motives of faith.

47 Q. Why must sorrow be supernatural?
A. Sorrow must be supernatural because the end to which it is directed is supernatural, namely, God's pardon, the acquisition of sanctifying grace, and the right to eternal glory.

48 Q. Explain more clearly the difference between natural and supernatural sorrow.
A. He who repents of having offended God because God is infinitely good and worthy of being loved for His own sake; of having lost Heaven and merited hell; or because of the intrinsic malice of sin, has supernatural sorrow, since all these are motives of faith. On the contrary, he who repents only because of the dishonour or chastisement inflicted by men, or because of some purely temporal loss, has a natural sorrow, since he repents from human motives alone.

49 Q. Why must sorrow be supreme?
A. Sorrow must be supreme because we must look upon and

The Sacraments

hate sin as the greatest of all evils, being as it is an offence against God.

50 Q. To have sorrow for sin, is it necessary to weep, as we sometimes do, in consequence of the misfortunes of this life?
A. It is not necessary to shed tears of sorrow for our sins; it is enough if in our heart we make more of having offended God than of any other misfortune whatsoever.

51 Q. What is meant by saying that sorrow must be universal?
A. It means that it must extend to every mortal sin committed.

52 Q. Why should sorrow extend to every mortal sin committed?
A. Because he who does not repent of even one mortal sin still remains an enemy to God.

53 Q. What should we do to have sorrow for our sins?
A. To have sorrow for our sins we should ask it of God with our whole heart, and excite it in ourselves by the thought of the great evil we have done by sinning.

54 Q. What should you do to excite yourself to detest your sins?
A. To excite myself to detest my sins:
- (1) I will consider the rigour of the infinite justice of God and the foulness of sin which has defiled my soul and made me worthy of the eternal punishment of hell;
- (2) I will consider that by sin I have lost the grace, friendship and sonship of God and the inheritance of Heaven;
- (3) That I have offended my Redeemer who died for me and that my sins caused His death;
- (4) That I have despised my Creator and my God, that I have turned my back upon Him who is my Supreme

Good and worthy of being loved above everything else and of being faithfully served.

55 Q. In going to confession should we be extremely solicitous to have a true sorrow for our sins?
A. In going to confession we should certainly be very solicitous to have a true sorrow for our sins, because this is of all things the most important; and if sorrow is wanting the confession is no good.

56 Q. If one has only venial sins to confess, must he be sorry for all of them?
A. If one has only venial sins to confess it is enough to repent of some of them for his confession to be valid; but to obtain pardon of all of them it is necessary to repent of all he remembers having committed.

57 Q. If one has only venial sins to confess and if he does not repent of even one of them, does he make a good confession?
A. If one confesses only venial sins without having sorrow for at least one of them, his confession is in vain; moreover it would be sacrilegious if the absence of sorrow was conscious.

58 Q. What should be done to render the confession of only venial sins more secure?
A. To render the confession of venial sins more secure it is prudent also to confess with true sorrow some grave sin of the past, even though it has been already confessed.

59 Q. Is it well to make an act of contrition often?
A. It is well and most useful to make an act of contrition often, especially before going to sleep or when we know we have or fear we have fallen into mortal sin, in order to recover God's grace as soon as possible; and this practice will make it easier for us to obtain from God the grace of making a like act at time of our greatest need, that is, when in danger of death.

The Sacraments

Resolution of Sinning No More

60 Q. In what does a good resolution consist?
A. A good resolution consists in a determined will not to commit sin for the future and to use all necessary means to avoid it.

61 Q. What conditions should a resolution have in order to be good?
A. A resolution, inordertobe good, should have three principal conditions: It ought to be absolute, universal, and efficacious.

62 Q. What is meant by an absolute resolution?
A. It means that the resolution ought to be without any restrictions of time, place or person.

63 Q. What is meant by a universal resolution?
A. It means that we should avoid all mortal sins, both those already committed as well as those which we can possibly commit.

64 Q. What is meant by an efficacious resolution?
A. It means that there must be a determined will to lose everything rather than commit another sin; to avoid the dangerous occasions of sin; to stamp out our bad habits; and to discharge the obligations that may have been contracted in consequence of our sins.

65 Q. What is meant by a bad habit?
A. By a bad habit is meant an acquired disposition to fall easily into those sins to which we have become accustomed.

66 Q. What must be done to correct bad habits?
A. To correct bad habits we must watch over ourselves, pray much, go often to confession, have one good director, and put into practice the counsels and remedies which he gives us.

67 Q. What is meant by dangerous occasions of sin?
A. By dangerous occasions of sin are meant all those cir-

cumstances of time, place, person, or things, which, of their very nature or because of our frailty, lead us to commit sin.

68 Q. Are we strictly bound to shun dangerous occasions?
A. We are strictly bound to shun those dangerous occasions which ordinarily lead us to commit mortal sin, and which are called the proximate occasions of sin.

69 Q. What should a person do who cannot avoid a certain occasion of sin?
A. A person who cannot avoid a certain occasion of sin should lay the matter before his confessor and follow his advice.

70 Q. What considerations will help us to make a good resolution?
A. The same considerations help us to make a good resolution as are efficacious in exciting sorrow; that is, a consideration of the motives we have to fear God's justice and to love His infinite goodness.

The Accusation of Sins to the Confessor

71 Q. Having prepared properly for confession by an examination of conscience, by exciting sorrow, and by forming a good resolution, what do you do next?
A. Having prepared properly for confession by an examination of conscience, by sorrow, and by a purpose of amendment, I will go to make an accusation of my sins to the confessor in order to get absolution.

72 Q. What sins are we bound to confess?
A. We are bound to confess all our mortal sins; it is well, however, to confess our venial sins also.

73 Q. Which are the qualities the accusation of sins, or confession, ought to have?
A. The principal qualities which the accusation of our sins

The Sacraments

ought to have are five: It ought to be humble, entire, sincere, prudent and brief.

74 Q. What is meant by saying that the accusation ought to be humble?
A. That the accusation ought to be humble, means that the penitent should accuse himself to his confessor without pride or boasting; but with the feelings of one who is guilty, who confesses his guilt, and who appears before his judge.

75 Q. What is meant by saying that the accusation ought to be entire?
A. That the accusation ought to be entire means that all mortal sins we are conscious of having committed since our last good confession must be made known, together with the circumstances and number.

76 Q. What circumstances must be made known for the accusation to be entire?
A. For the accusation to be entire, the circumstances which change the species of the sin must be made known.

77 Q. Which are the circumstances which change the species of a sin?
A. The circumstances which change the species of a sin are:
(1) Those by which a sinful action from being venial becomes mortal;
(2) Those by means of which a sinful action contains the malice of two or more mortal sins.

78 Q. Give an example of a circumstance making a venial sin mortal.
A. If, to excuse himself, a man were to tell a lie and by doing so occasion serious harm to another, he would be bound to make known this circumstance, which changes the lie from an officious lie to a seriously harmful lie.

79 Q. Give an example of a circumstance on account of which a single sinful action contains the malice of two or more sins.
A. If a man were to steal a sacred object he would be bound to accuse himself of this circumstance which adds to the theft the malice of sacrilege.

80 Q. If a penitent is not certain of having committed a sin must he confess it?
A. If a penitent is not certain of having committed a sin he is not bound to confess it; and if he does confess it, he should add that he is not certain of having committed it.

81 Q. What should he do who does not remember the exact number of his sins?
A. He who does not distinctly remember the number of his sins must mention the number as nearly as he can.

82 Q. Does he who through forgetfulness does not confess a mortal sin, or a necessary circumstance, make a good confession?
A. He who through pure forgetfulness does not confess a mortal sin, or a necessary circumstance, makes a good confession, provided he has been duly diligent in trying to remember it.

83 Q. If a mortal sin, forgotten in confession, is afterwards remembered, are we bound to confess it in another confession?
A. If a mortal sin forgotten in confession is afterwards remembered we are certainly bound to confess it the next time we go to confession.

84 Q. What does he commit who, through shame or some other motive, wilfully conceals a mortal sin in confession?
A. He who, through shame or some other motive, wilfully conceals a mortal sin in confession, profanes the sacrament and is consequently guilty of a very great sacrilege.

The Sacraments

85 Q. In what way must he relieve his conscience who has wilfully concealed a mortal sin in confession?
A. He who has wilfully concealed a mortal sin in confession, must reveal to his confessor the sin concealed, say in how many confessions he has concealed it, and make all these confessions over again, from the last good confession.

86 Q. What reflection should a penitent make who is tempted to conceal a sin in confession?
A. He who is tempted to conceal a mortal sin in confession should reflect:
- (1) That he was not ashamed to sin, in the presence of God who sees all;
- (2) That it is better to manifest his sin secretly to the confessor than to live tormented by sin, die an unhappy death, and be covered with shame before the whole world on the day of general judgment;
- (3) That the confessor is bound by the seal of confession under the gravest sin and under threat of the severest punishments both temporal and eternal.

87 Q. What is meant by saying that the accusation ought to be sincere?
A. By saying that the accusation ought to be sincere, is meant that we must unfold our sins as they are, without excusing them, lessening them, or increasing them.

88 Q. What is meant by saying that the confession ought to be prudent?
A. That the confession ought to be prudent, means that in confessing our sins we should use the most careful words possible and be on our guard against revealing the sins of others.

89 Q. What is meant by saying the confession ought to be short?
A. That the confession ought to be short, means that we should say nothing that is useless for the purpose of confession.

90 Q. Is it not a heavy burden to be obliged to confess one's sins to another, especially when these are shameful sins?
A. Although it may be a heavy burden to confess one's sins to another, still it must be done, because it is of divine precept, and because pardon can be obtained in no other way; and, moreover, because the difficulty is compensated by many advantages and great consolations.

How to Make a Good Confession

91 Q. How do you present yourself to the confessor?
A. I kneel at the feet of the confessor and I say: "Bless me, Father, for I have sinned."

92 Q. What do you do while the confessor blesses you?
A. I humbly bow my head to receive the blessing and I make the Sign of the Cross.

93 Q. Having made the sign of the Cross what should you say?
A. Having made the sign of the Cross, I say: "I confess to Almighty God, to blessed Mary ever Virgin, to all the Saints, and to you, my spiritual Father, that I have sinned."

94 Q. And then what must you say?
A. Then I must say: "I was at confession such a time; by the grace of God I received absolution, performed my penance, and went to Holy Communion." Then I accuse myself of my sins.

95 Q. When you have finished the accusation of your sins what do you do?
A. When I have finished the accusation of my sins I say: "I accuse myself also of all the sins of my past life, especially of

those against such or such a virtue"—for example, against purity or against the Fourth Commandment, etc.

96 Q. After this accusation what should you say?
A. I should say: "For all these sins and for those I do not remember, I ask pardon of God with my whole heart, and penance and absolution of you, my spiritual Father."

97 Q. Having thus finished the accusation of your sins what remains to be done?
A. Having finished the accusation of my sins I should listen respectfully to what the confessor says, accept the penance with a sincere intention of performing it; and, from my heart, renew my act of contrition while he gives me absolution.

98 Q. Having received absolution what remains to be done?
A. Having received absolution I should thank the Lord, perform my penance as soon as possible, and put in practice the advice of the confessor.

Absolution

99 Q. Must confessors always give absolution to those who go to confession to them?
A. Confessors should give absolution to those only whom they judge properly disposed to receive it.

100 Q. May confessors sometimes defer or refuse absolution?
A. Confessors not only may, but must defer or refuse absolution in certain cases so as not to profane the sacrament.

101 Q. Who are those penitents who are to be accounted badly disposed and to whom absolution must as a rule be refused or deferred?
A. Penitents who are to be accounted badly disposed are chiefly the following:
(1) Those who do not know the principal mysteries of

their faith, or who neglect to learn those other truths of Christian Doctrine which they are bound to know according to their state;

(2) Those who are gravely negligent in examining their conscience, who show no signs of sorrow or repentance;

(3) Those who are able but not willing to restore the goods of others, or the reputations they have injured;

(4) Those who do not from their heart forgive their enemies;

(5) Those who will not practise the means necessary to correct their bad habits;

(6) Those who will not abandon the proximate occasions of sin.

102 Q. Is not a confessor too severe, who defers absolution because he does not believe the penitent is well enough disposed?

A. A confessor who defers absolution because he does not believe the penitent well enough disposed, is not too severe; on the contrary, he is very charitable and acts as a good physician who tries all remedies, even those that are disagreeable and painful, to save the life of his patient.

103 Q. Should the sinner to whom absolution is deferred or refused, despair or leave off going to confession altogether?

A. A sinner to whom absolution is deferred or refused, should not despair or leave off going to confession altogether; he should, on the contrary, humble himself, acknowledge his deplorable state, profit by the good advice his confessor gives him, and thus put himself as soon as possible in a state deserving of absolution.

The Sacraments

104 Q. What should a penitent do with regard to selecting a confessor?
A. A genuine penitent should earnestly recommend himself to God for help to enable him to select a pious, learned, and prudent confessor, into whose hands he should put himself, obeying him as his judge and physician.

Satisfaction or Penance

105 Q. What is satisfaction?
A. Satisfaction, which is also called sacramental penance, is one of the acts of the penitent by which he makes a certain reparation to the justice of God for his sins, by performing the works the confessor imposes on him.

106 Q. Is the penitent bound to accept the penance imposed on him by the confessor?
A. Yes, the penitent is bound to accept the penance imposed on him by the confessor if he can perform it; and if he cannot, he should humbly say so, and ask some other penance.

107 Q. When should the penance be performed?
A. If the confessor has fixed no time, the penance should be performed as soon as convenient, and as far as possible while in the state of grace.

108 Q. How should the penance be performed?
A. The penance should be performed entirely and devoutly.

109 Q. Why is a penance imposed in confession?
A. A penance is imposed because, after sacramental absolution which remits sin and its eternal punishment, there generally remains a temporal punishment to be undergone, either in this world or in Purgatory.

110 Q. Why has our Lord willed to remit all the punishment due to sin in the sacrament of Baptism, and not in the sacrament of Penance?
A. Our Lord has willed to remit all the punishment due to sin in the sacrament of Baptism, and not in the sacrament of Penance, because the sins after Baptism are much more grievous, being committed with fuller knowledge and greater ingratitude for God's benefits, and also in order that the obligation of satisfying for them may restrain us from falling into sin again.

111 Q. Can we of ourselves make satisfaction to God?
A. Of ourselves we cannot make satisfaction to God, but we certainly can do so by uniting ourselves to Jesus Christ, who gives value to our actions by the merits of His passion and death.

112 Q. Does the penance which the confessor imposes always suffice to discharge the punishment which remains due to our sins?
A. The penance which the confessor imposes does not ordinarily suffice to discharge the punishment remaining due to our sins; and hence we must try to supply it by other voluntary penances.

113 Q. Which are the works of penance?
A. The works of penance may be reduced to three kinds: Prayer, Fasting, and Alms-deeds.

114 Q. What is meant by prayer?
A. By prayer is meant every kind of pious exercise.

115 Q. What is meant by fasting?
A. By fasting is meant every kind of mortification.

116 Q. What is meant by almsgiving?
A. By almsgiving is meant every spiritual or corporal work of mercy.

The Sacraments

117 Q. Which penance is the more meritorious, that which the confessor gives, or that which we do of our own choice?
A. The penance which the confessor imposes is the most meritorious, because being part of the sacrament it receives greater virtue from the merits of the passion of Jesus Christ.

118 Q. Do those who die after having received absolution but before they have fully satisfied the justice of God, go straight to Heaven?
A. No, they go to Purgatory there to satisfy the justice of God and be perfectly purified.

119 Q. Can the souls in Purgatory be relieved of their pains by us?
A. Yes, the souls in Purgatory can be relieved by our prayers, alms-deeds, all our other good works, and by indulgences, but above all by the Holy Sacrifice of the Mass.

120 Q. Besides his penance, what else must the penitent do after confession?
A. Besides performing his penance after confession, the penitent, if he has justly injured another in his goods or reputation, or if he has given him scandal, must as soon as possible, and as far as he is able, restore him his goods, repair his honour, and remedy the scandal.

121 Q. How can the scandal given be remedied?
A. The scandal given can be remedied by removing the occasion of it and by edifying by word and example those whom we have scandalised.

122 Q. How should we make satisfaction to one whom we have offended?
A. We should make satisfaction to one whom we have offended, by asking his pardon, or by some other suitable reparation.

123 Q. What fruits does a good confession produce in us?
A. A good confession:
- (1) Remits the sins we have committed and gives us the grace of God;
- (2) Restores us peace and quiet of conscience;
- (3) Reopens the gates of Heaven and changes the eternal punishment of hell into a temporal punishment;
- (4) Preserves us from falling again, and renders us capable of partaking of the treasury of Indulgences.

Indulgences

124 Q. What is an Indulgence?
A. An Indulgence is the remission of the temporal punishment due on account of our sins which have been already pardoned as far as their guilt is concerned—a remission accorded by the Church outside the sacrament of Penance.

125 Q. From whom has the Church received the power to grant Indulgences?
A. The Church has received the power to grant Indulgences from Jesus Christ.

126 Q. In what way does the Church by means of Indulgences remit this temporal punishment?
A. The Church by means of Indulgences remits this temporal punishment by applying to us the superabundant merits of Jesus Christ, of the Blessed Virgin and of the Saints, which constitute what is known as the Treasure of the Church.

127 Q. Who has the power to grant Indulgences?
A. The Pope alone has the power to grant Indulgences in the whole Church, and the Bishop in his own diocese, according to the faculty given him by the Pope.

The Sacraments

128 Q. How many kinds of Indulgences are there?
A. Indulgences are of two kinds: plenary and partial.

129 Q. What is a plenary Indulgence?
A. A plenary Indulgence is that by which the whole temporal punishment due to our sins is remitted. Hence, if one were to die after having gained such an Indulgence, he would go straight to Heaven, being, as he is, perfectly exempt from the pains of Purgatory.

130 Q. What is a partial Indulgence?
A. A partial Indulgence is that by which is remitted only a part of the temporal punishment due to our sins.

131 Q. Why does the Church grant Indulgences?
A. In granting Indulgences the Church intends to aid our incapacity to expiate all the temporal punishment in this world, by enabling us to obtain by means of works of piety and Christian charity that which in the first ages Christians gained by the rigour of Canonical penances.

132 Q. What is meant by an Indulgence of forty or a hundred days or of seven years, and the like?
A. By an Indulgence of forty or a hundred days, or of seven years and the like, is meant the remission of so much of the temporal punishment as would have been paid by penances of forty or a hundred days, or seven years, anciently prescribed in the Church.

133 Q. What value should we set on Indulgences?
A. We should set the greatest value on Indulgences because by them we satisfy the justice of God and obtain possession of Heaven sooner and more easily.

134 Q. Which are the conditions necessary to gain Indulgences?
A. The conditions necessary to gain Indulgences are:
  (1) The state of grace (at least at the final completion of

the work), and freedom from those venial faults, the punishment of which we wish to cancel;

(2) The fulfilment of all the works the Church enjoins in order to gain the Indulgence;

(3) The intention to gain it.

135 Q. Can Indulgences be applied also to the souls in Purgatory?
A. Yes, Indulgences can be applied also to the souls in Purgatory, when he who grants them says that they may be so applied.

136 Q. What is a Jubilee?
A. A Jubilee, which as a rule is granted every twenty-five years, is a Plenary Indulgence to which are attached many privileges and special concessions, such as that of being able to obtain absolution from certain reserved sins and from censures, and the commutation of certain vows.

The Sacrament of Extreme Unction

1 Q. What is Extreme Unction?
A. Extreme Unction is a sacrament instituted for the spiritual as well as for the temporal comfort of the sick in danger of death.

2 Q. What are the effects of Extreme Unction?
A. The sacrament of Extreme Unction produces the following effects:
   (1) It increases sanctifying grace;
   (2) It remits venial sins, and also mortal sins which the sick person, if contrite, is unable to confess;
   (3) It takes away weakness and sloth which remain even after pardon has been obtained;
   (4) It gives strength to bear illness patiently, to withstand;
   (5) It aids in restoring us to health of body if it is for the good of the soul.

The Sacraments

3 Q. When should Extreme Unction be received?
A. Extreme Unction should be received when the illness is dangerous, and after the sick person has received, if possible, the sacraments of Penance and the Blessed Eucharist; it is even well to receive it while he has the use of his senses, and has still some hope of recovery.

4 Q. Why is it well to receive Extreme Unction when the sick person has still the use of his senses, and has still some hope of recovery?
A. It is well to receive Extreme Unction while the sick person retains the use of his senses, and while there remains some hope of his recovery because:
  (1) He thus receives it with better dispositions, and is hence able to derive greater fruit from it;
  (2) This sacrament restores health of body (should it be for the good of the soul) by assisting the powers of nature; and hence it should not be deferred until recovery is despaired of.

5 Q. With what dispositions should the sacrament of Extreme Unction be received?
A. The principal dispositions for receiving Extreme Unction are: To be in the state of grace; to have confidence in the power of this sacrament and in the mercy of God and to be resigned to the will of the Lord.

6 Q. What should be the sick person's feelings on seeing the priest?
A. On seeing the priest, the sick person should feel thankful to God for having sent him; and should gladly receive the comforts of religion, which, if he is able, he should request himself.

The Sacrament of Holy Orders

1 Q. What is the sacrament of Holy Orders?
A. Holy Orders is a sacrament which gives power to exercise the sacred duties connected with the worship of God and the salvation of souls, and which imprints the character of Minister of God on the soul of him who receives it.

2 Q. Why is it called Orders?
A. It is called Orders because it comprises various grades, the one subordinate to the other, from which the sacred Hierarchy is composed.

3 Q. Which are these grades?
A. The highest is the Episcopate, which contains the fullness of the Priesthood; then comes the Priesthood; then the Diaconate, the Sub-diaconate, and the Orders called Minor.

4 Q. When did Jesus Christ institute the Sacerdotal Order?
A. Jesus Christ instituted the Sacerdotal Order at the Last Supper when he conferred on the Apostles and their successors the power of consecrating the Blessed Eucharist. Then on the day of His resurrection He conferred on them the power of remitting and retaining sin, thus constituting them the first Priests of the New Law in all the fullness of their power.

5 Q. Who is the Minister of this sacrament?
A. The bishop is the Minister of this sacrament.

6 Q. Is the dignity of the Christian Priesthood a great dignity?
A. The dignity of the Christian Priesthood is great indeed, because of the two-fold power which Jesus Christ has conferred upon it—that over His real body and that over His mystical body, or the Church; and because of the divine mission committed to priests to lead men to eternal life.

The Sacraments

7 Q. Is the Catholic Priesthood necessary in the Church?
A. The Catholic Priesthood is necessary in the Church, because without it the faithful would be deprived of the Holy Sacrifice of the Mass and of the greater part of the sacraments; they would have no one to instruct them in the faith; and they would be as sheep without a shepherd, a prey to wolves; in short, the Church, such as Christ instituted it, would no longer exist.

8 Q. Will the Catholic Priesthood therefore never cease on this earth?
A. In spite of the war that hell wages against it, the Catholic Priesthood will last until the end of time, because Jesus Christ has promised that the powers of hell shall never prevail against His Church.

9 Q. Is it a sin to despise Priests?
A. It is a very grave sin, because the scorn and insults cast on Priests fall upon Jesus Christ Himself, who said to His Apostles: He who despises you, despises Me.

10 Q. What motive should he have who embraces the ecclesiastical state?
A. The motive of one who embraces the ecclesiastical state should be the glory of God and the salvation of souls alone.

11 Q. What is necessary to enter the ecclesiastical state?
A. To enter the ecclesiastical state a divine vocation is necessary before all else.

12 Q. What should be done to find out whether God calls us to the ecclesiastical state?
A. To find out if God calls us to the ecclesiastical state we should:
    (1) Fervently pray the Lord to make known His will to us;
    (2) Consult our Bishop or a learned and prudent director;
    (3) Diligently examine whether we have the capacity

necessary for the studies, the duties, and the obligations of this state.

13 Q. If one were to enter the ecclesiastical state without a divine vocation would he do wrong?
A. If one were to enter the ecclesiastical state without a divine vocation he would commit a great wrong and run the risk of being lost.

14 Q. Do those parents sin who, from worldly motives, impel their sons to embrace the ecclesiastical state without any vocation?
A. Those parents who, for worldly motives, impel their sons to embrace the ecclesiastical state without any vocation commit a very grave sin, because by thus acting they usurp the right God has reserved to Himself alone of choosing His own ministers; and they expose their children to the danger of eternal damnation.

15 Q. Which are the duties of the faithful towards those who are called to Holy Orders?
A. The faithful should:
    (1) Give their children and dependents full liberty to follow the call of God;
    (2) Pray God to deign to grant good pastors and zealous ministers to His Church—it is precisely for this end that the fasts of Quarter Tense have been instituted;
    (3) Have special respect for all who are consecrated by Holy Orders to God's service.

The Sacrament of Matrimony

Nature of the Sacrament of Matrimony

1 Q. What is the sacrament of Matrimony?
A. Matrimony is a sacrament, instituted by our Lord Jesus Christ, which creates a holy and indissoluble union between a man and woman, and gives them grace to love one another holily and to bring up their children as Christians.

2 Q. By whom was Matrimony instituted?
A. Matrimony was instituted by God Himself in the Garden of Paradise, and was raised to the dignity of a sacrament by Jesus Christ in the New Law.

3 Q. Has the sacrament of Matrimony any special signification?
A. The sacrament of Matrimony signifies the indissoluble union of Jesus Christ with the Church, His Spouse, and our holy Mother.

4 Q. Why do we say that the bond of marriage is indissoluble?

A. We say that the bond of marriage is indissoluble or that it cannot be dissolved except by the death of either husband or wife, because God so ordained from the beginning and so Jesus Christ our Lord solemnly proclaimed.

5 Q. Can the contract be separated from the sacrament in Christian marriage?
A. No, in marriage among Christians the contract cannot be separated from the sacrament, because, for Christians, marriage is nothing else than the natural contract itself, raised by Jesus Christ to the dignity of a sacrament.

6 Q. Among Christians, then, there can be no true marriage that is not a sacrament?
A. Among Christians there can be no true marriage that is not a sacrament.

7 Q. What effects does the sacrament of Matrimony produce?
A. The sacrament of matrimony:
    (1) Gives an increase of sanctifying grace;
    (2) Gives a special grace for the faithful discharge of all the duties of the married state.

Minister—Rite—Dispositions

8 Q. Who are the Ministers of this sacrament?
A. The Ministers of this sacrament are the couple themselves, who together confer and receive the sacrament.

9 Q. How is this sacrament administered?
A. This sacrament, preserving, as it does, the nature of a contract, is administered by the contracting parties themselves, who declare, in the presence of the parish priest, or another priest delegated by him, and of two witnesses, that they take each other in marriage.

10 Q. What use, then, is the blessing which the parish priest gives to the married couple?
A. The blessing which the parish priest gives to the married couple is not necessary to constitute the sacrament, but it is given to sanction their union in the name of the Church and to invoke on them more abundantly the blessing of God.

11 Q. What intention should those have who contract marriage?
A. Those who contract marriage should have the intention:
    (1) Of doing the will of God, who calls them to that state;

The Sacraments

(2) Of working out in that state the salvation of their souls;

(3) Of bringing up their children as Christians, if God should bless them with any.

12 Q. How should those about to be married prepare themselves to receive this sacrament with fruit?
A. In order to receive this sacrament with fruit, those about to be married should:
   (1) Earnestly recommend themselves to God, so as to know His will and obtain the graces necessary for that state;
   (2) Consult their parents before making any promise, because obedience and the respect due to them demand this;
   (3) Prepare themselves by a good confession, or, if necessary, a general confession of their whole life;
   (4) Avoid all dangerous familiarity in word or act while in each other's company.

13 Q. Which are the principal obligations of married persons?
A. Married persons should:
   (1) Guard inviolably their conjugal fidelity and behave always and in all things as Christians;
   (2) Love one another, bear patiently with one another, and live in peace and concord;
   (3) Think seriously of providing for their children, if they have any, according to their needs; bring them up as Christians, and leave them free to choose the state of life to which they are called by God.

Conditions and Impediments

14 Q. What is necessary to contract Christian marriage validly?
A. To contract Christian marriage validly it is necessary to be free from every diriment impediment to marriage; and to give consent freely to the marriage contract in the presence of the parish priest (or a priest delegated by him) and of two witnesses.

15 Q. What is necessary to contract marriage lawfully?
A. To contract marriage lawfully it is necessary to be free from every impeding impediment to marriage; to be instructed in the principal truths of religion; and, finally, to be in a state of grace; otherwise a sacrilege would be committed.

16 Q. What are impediments to marriage?
A. Impediments to marriage are certain circumstances which render marriage either invalid or unlawful. The former are called diriment impediments and the latter impeding impediments.

17 Q. Give examples of diriment impediments.
A. Diriment impediments are, for example, relationship to the fourth degree,[7] spiritual relationship, a solemn vow of chastity, or difference in religion, that is, when one party is baptised and the other is not.

18 Q. Give examples of impeding impediments.
A. Impeding impediments are, for example, the forbidden times, a simple vow of chastity, and the like.

---

[7] First degree = brothers and sisters; second degree = first cousins; third degree = second cousins; fourth degree = third cousins. [The new Code of Canon Law (1983) reduced this impediment to first cousins: Can. 1091 & 108]

The Sacraments

19 Q. Are the faithful obliged to make known to ecclesiastical authority impediments of which they have a knowledge?
A. The faithful are obliged to make known to ecclesiastical authority impediments of which they have knowledge; and for this reason the names of those who intend to get married are published in the Church.

20 Q. Who has the power to regulate impediments to marriage, to dispense from them, and to judge of the validity of Christian marriage?
A. The Church alone has power to regulate impediments to marriage, to judge of the validity of marriage among Christians and to dispense from the impediments which she has placed.

21 Q. Why has the Church alone power to place impediments and to judge of the validity of marriage?
A. The Church alone has power to place impediments, to judge of the validity of marriage, and to dispense from the impediments which she has placed, because the contract, being inseparable from the sacrament in a Christian marriage, also comes under the power of the Church, to which alone Jesus Christ gave the right to make laws and give decisions in sacred things.

22 Q. Can the civil authority dissolve the bonds of Christian marriage by divorce?
A. No, the bond of Christian marriage cannot be dissolved by the civil authority, because the civil authority cannot interfere with the matter of the sacrament nor can it put asunder what God has joined together.

23 Q. What is a civil marriage?
A. It is nothing but a mere formality prescribed by the [civil] law to give and insure the civil effects of the marriage to the spouses and their children.

24 Q. Is it sufficient for a Christian to get only the civil marriage or contract?
A. For a Christian, it is not sufficient to get only the civil contract, because it is not a sacrament, and therefore not a true marriage.

25 Q. In what condition would the spouses be who would live together united only by a civil marriage?
A. Spouses who would live together united by only a civil marriage would be in an habitual state of mortal sin, and their union would always be illegitimate in the sight of God and of the Church.

26 Q. Should we also get the civil marriage?
A. We should perform the civil marriage, because, though it is not a sacrament, it provides the spouses and their children with the civil effects of conjugal society; for this reason, the ecclesiastical authority as a general rule allows the religious marriage only after the formalities prescribed by the civil authorities have been accomplished.[8]

---

[8] In many countries, especially English speaking countries, the civil authority acknowledges the religious marriage and gives it the civil effects, thus there is no need of a separate ceremony. However the states often add certain requirements and formalities which should be observed.

On the Commandments of God and of the Church

The Commandments of God in General

1 Q. What is treated of in the third part of Christian Doctrine?
A. The Commandments of God and of the Church are treated of in the third part of Christian Doctrine.

2 Q. How many Commandments of God's Law are there?
A. There are Ten Commandments of God's Law:
  I am the Lord thy God:
  1. Thou shalt not have strange gods before Me;
  2. Thou shalt not take the Name of the Lord thy God in vain;
  3. Remember thou keep holy the Sabbath Day;
  4. Honour thy Father and thy Mother;
  5. Thou shalt not kill;
  6. Thou shalt not commit adultery;
  7. Thou shalt not steal;
  8. Thou shalt not bear false witness;
  9. Thou shalt not covet another's wife;
  10. Thou shalt not covet another's goods.

3 Q. Why are the Commandments of God so named?
A. The Commandments of God are so named because God Himself has stamped them on the soul of every man; promulgated them, engraved on two tables of stone, on Mount Sinai, in the Old Law; and Jesus Christ has confirmed them in the New Law.

4 Q. Which are the Commandments of the first table?
A. The Commandments of the first table are the first three, which directly regard God and our duties towards Him.

5 Q. Which are the Commandments of the second table?
A. The Commandments of the second table are the last seven, which regard our neighbour, and our duties towards him.

6 Q. Are we bound to observe the Commandments?
A. Yes, we are bound to observe the Commandments, because we are all bound to live according to the will of God who created us, and because a serious transgression against even one of them is enough to merit hell.

7 Q. Are we able to observe the Commandments?
A. Yes, without doubt we are able to observe God's Commandments, because God never commands anything that is impossible, and because He gives grace to observe them to those who ask it as they should.

8 Q. What, in a general way, should we consider in each of the Commandments?
A. In each of the Commandments we should consider its positive part and its negative part, that is, what it commands and what it forbids.

The First Commandment

1 Q. Why is it said at the commencement of the Commandments: *I am the Lord thy God?*
A. It is said at the commencement of the Commandments: *I am the Lord thy God,* to show us that God being our Creator and Lord, can command whatever He wills, and that we, being His creatures, are bound to obey Him.

The Commandments of God in General

2 Q. In the words of the First Commandment: *Thou shalt not have strange gods before Me,* **what does God command us?**
A. By the words of the First Commandment: *Thou shalt not have strange gods before Me,* He commands us to acknowledge, adore, love and serve Him alone as our Sovereign Lord.

3 Q. How do we fulfil the First Commandment?
A. We fulfil the First Commandment by the practice of internal and external worship.

4 Q. What is internal worship?
A. Internal worship is the honour which is given to God with the faculties of the soul alone, that is with the intellect and the will.

5 Q. What is external worship?
A. External worship is the homage that is given to God by means of outward acts and of sensible objects.

6 Q. Is it not enough internally to adore God with the heart alone?
A. No, it is not enough internally to adore God with the heart alone; we must also adore Him externally with both soul and body, because He is the Creator and absolute Lord of both.

7 Q. Can there be external worship without internal worship?

A. No, in no way can there be external worship without internal, because unless external worship is accompanied by internal, it is destitute of life, of merit, and of efficacy, like a body without a soul.

8 Q. What is forbidden by the First Commandment?
A. The First Commandment forbids idolatry, superstition, sacrilege, heresy, and every other sin against religion.

9 Q. What is idolatry?
A. Idolatry is the giving to any creature, for example, to a statue, to an image, or to a man, the supreme worship of adoration that belongs to God alone.

10 Q. How is this prohibition expressed in Holy Scripture?
A. This prohibition is expressed in Holy Scripture in these words: Thou shalt not make to thyself a graven thing, nor the likeness of anything that is in heaven above, or on the earth beneath; and thou shalt not adore them or serve them.

11 Q. Do these words forbid every kind of image?
A. Certainly not; but only those of false divinities, made to be adored, as idolaters adore them. So true is this, that God Himself commanded Moses to make images, as, for example, the two statues of the Cherubim for the Ark, and the Brazen Serpent in the desert.

12 Q. What is superstition?
A. Superstition is any devotion that is contrary to the teaching and practice of the Church; as also the ascribing to any action or any thing whatever a supernatural virtue which it does not possess.

13 Q. What is a sacrilege?
A. A sacrilege is the profanation of a place, of a person, or of a thing consecrated to God and set apart for his worship.

14 Q. What is heresy?
A. Heresy is a culpable error of the intellect by which some truth of faith is obstinately denied.

15 Q. What else does the First Commandment forbid?
A. The First Commandment also forbids all dealings with the devil, and all association with anti-Christian sects.

The Commandments of God in General

16 Q. If one were to have recourse to and invoke the devil, would he commit a grave sin?
A. If one were to have recourse to and invoke the devil, he would commit an enormous sin, because the devil is the most wicked enemy both of God and of man.

17 Q. Is it lawful to put questions to speaking or writing tables or in any way to consult the souls of the dead by means of spiritism?
A. All the practices of spiritism are unlawful, because they are superstitious; and often they are not free from diabolical intervention; and hence they are rightly condemned by the Church.

18 Q. Does the First Commandment forbid us to honour and invoke the Angels and Saints?
A. No, it is not forbidden to honour and invoke the Angels and Saints; on the contrary, we should do so, because it is a good and useful practice highly commended by the Church; for they are God's friends and our intercessors with Him.

19 Q. Since Jesus Christ is our only mediator with God, why have recourse also to the intercession of the Blessed Virgin and the Saints?
A. Jesus Christ is our Mediator with God, because being true God and true man He alone in virtue of His own merits has reconciled us to God and obtains us all graces. But in virtue of the merits of Jesus Christ, and through the charity which unites them to God and us, the Blessed Virgin and the Saints help us by their intercession to obtain the graces we ask. And this is one of the great benefits of the Communion of Saints.

20 Q. May we also honour the sacred images of Jesus Christ and of the Saints?
A. Yes, because the honour we give the sacred images of Jesus Christ and of the Saints is referred to their very persons.

21 Q. May the relics of the Saints be honoured?
A. Yes, we should honour the relics of the Saints, because their bodies were living members of Jesus Christ and temples of the Holy Ghost, and will rise gloriously to eternal life.

22 Q. What is the difference between the honour we give to God and the honour we give to the Saints?
A. Between the honour we give to God and the honour we give to the Saints there is this difference, that we adore God because of his infinite excellence, whereas we do not adore the Saints, but honour and venerate them as God's friends and our intercessors with Him. The honour we give to God is called **Latria**, that is, the worship of adoration; the honour we give to the Saints is called **Dulia**, that is, the veneration of the servants of God; while the special honour we give to the Blessed Virgin is called **Hyperdulia**, that is, a special veneration of the Mother of God.

The Second Commandment

1 Q. What does the Second Commandment: *Thou shalt not take the Name of God in vain,* forbid?
A. The Second Commandment: *Thou shalt not take the Name of God in vain,* forbids us:
    (1) To utter the Name of God irreverently;
    (2) To blaspheme God, the Blessed Virgin or the Saints;
    (3) To take false, unnecessary, or unlawful oaths.

2 Q. What is meant by: *Not to utter the Name of God irreverently*?
A. *Not to utter the Name of God irreverently* means not to mention this Holy Name, or any other name that in a special way refers to God Himself, such as the name of Jesus, of Mary and the Saints, in anger or in joke or in any irreverent way whatsoever.

The Commandments of God in General

3 Q. What is blasphemy?
A. Blasphemy is a horrible sin which consists in words or acts of contempt or malediction against God, the Blessed Virgin, the Saints, or sacred things.

4 Q. Is there any difference between blasphemy and imprecation?
A. There is a difference, because by blasphemy one wishes evil to or curses God, the Blessed Virgin or the Saints; while by imprecation one wishes evil to or curses one's self or one's neighbour.

5 Q. What is an oath?
A. An oath is the calling on God to witness the truth of what one says or promises.

6 Q. Is it always forbidden to take an oath?
A. It is not always forbidden to take an oath; an oath is lawful and even gives honour to God, when it is necessary, and when one swears with truth, judgement and justice.

7 Q. When is an oath without truth?
A. When one affirms on oath what he knows or believes to be false, or when one promises under oath to do what one has no intention of doing.

8 Q. When is an oath without judgement?
A. When one makes oaths imprudently and without mature consideration, or in trivial matters.

9 Q. When is an oath without justice?
A. When one makes an oath to do something unjust or unlawful, as, for example, to swear to take revenge, or to steal, and so on.

10 Q. Are we obliged to keep an oath to do unjust or unlawful things?
A. Not only are we not obliged, but we should sin by doing such things, because they are forbidden by the laws of God and of the Church.

11 Q. What sin does he commit who swears falsely?
A. He who swears falsely commits a mortal sin, because he grievously dishonours God, the Infinite Truth, by calling Him to witness what is false.

12 Q. What does the Second Commandment command us to do?
A. The Second Commandment commands us to honour the Holy Name of God as well as to keep our oaths and vows.

13 Q. What is a vow?
A. A vow is a promise made to God regarding something which is good, within our power, and better than its opposite, and to the keeping of which we bind ourselves just as if it had been commanded us.

14 Q. If the keeping of a vow were to become very difficult, in whole or in part, what is to be done?
A. Commutation or dispensation, may be sought from one's Bishop or from the Pope, according to the character of the vow.

15 Q. Is it a sin to break a vow?
A. It is a sin to break a vow and therefore we should not make vows without mature reflection, nor, as a rule, without the advice of our confessor or other prudent person, so as not to expose ourselves to the danger of sinning.

16 Q. May vows be made to our Lady and the Saints?
A. Vows are made to God alone; we may, however, promise God to do something in honour of our Lady or the Saints.

The Commandments of God in General

The Third Commandment

1 Q. What does the Third Commandment: *Remember thou keep holy the Sabbath day*, command us to do?
A. The Third Commandment: *Remember thou keep holy the Sabbath day,* commands us to honour God by acts of worship on festivals.

2 Q. What are festivals?
A. In the Old Law they were Saturdays and certain other days regarded as specially solemn by the Jews; in the New Law they are Sundays and other festivals instituted by the Church.

3 Q. Why is Sunday sanctified instead of Saturday in the New Law?
A. Sunday, which means the Lord's Day, was substituted for Saturday, because it was on that day that our Lord rose from the dead.

4 Q. What act of worship is commanded us on festivals?
A. We are commanded to assist devoutly at the Holy Sacrifice of the Mass.

5 Q. With what other good works does a good Christian sanctify festivals?
A. A good Christian sanctifies festivals:
  (1) By attending Christian Doctrine, sermons, and the Divine Office;
  (2) By frequently and devoutly receiving the sacraments of Penance and the Blessed Eucharist;
  (3) By the practice of prayer and works of Christian charity.

6 Q. What does the Third Commandment forbid?
A. The Third Commandment forbids servile works and any other works that hinder the worship of God.

7 Q. What servile works are forbidden on festivals?
A. The servile works forbidden on festivals are those works called manual, that is, those material works in which the body has more part than the mind, such, for instance, as are ordinarily done by servants, labourers, and artisans.

8 Q. What sin does one commit by working on festivals?
A. One commits a mortal sin by working on festivals; brevity of time, however, will excuse from grave sin.

9 Q. Is no servile work at all permitted on festivals?
A. On festivals those works are permitted which are necessary for life, or for the service of God; as well as those done for a grave reason, with leave, when possible, from the Pastor.

10 Q. Why is servile work forbidden on festivals?
A. Servile work is forbidden on festivals in order that we may the better attend to divine worship, and to the care of our souls; and to enable us to rest from toil. Hence innocent recreation is not forbidden.

11 Q. What else above all should we avoid on festivals?
A. We should above all avoid sin and whatever leads to sin, such as dangerous diversions and dangerous places of amusement.

The Fourth Commandment

1 Q. What does the Fourth Commandment: *Honour thy father and thy mother*, command?
A. The Fourth Commandment: *Honour thy father and thy mother,* commands us to respect our parents, obey them in all that is not sinful, and assist them in their temporal and spiritual needs.

The Commandments of God in General

2 Q. What does the Fourth Commandment forbid?
A. The Fourth Commandment forbids us to offend our parents by word or by deed or in any other way.

3 Q. What other persons does this Commandment include under the names of father and mother?
A. Under the names of father and mother this Commandment also includes all our superiors, both ecclesiastical and lay, whom we must consequently obey and respect.

4 Q. Whence are derived the authority of parents to command their children and the duty of children to obey their parents?
A. The authority possessed by parents to command their children and the obligation children are under to obey their parents, are derived from God who constituted and established family life in order that in it man might have the first helps that are necessary towards his spiritual and temporal well-being.

5 Q. Have parents any duties towards their children?
A. Parents are bound to love, support and maintain their children; to attend to their religious and secular education; to give them good example; to keep them from the occasions of sin; to correct their faults; and to help them to embrace the state to which God has called them.

6 Q. Has God given us an example of a perfect family?
A. God gave us an example of a perfect family in the Holy Family in which Jesus Christ lived subject to the Blessed Virgin and St. Joseph until His thirtieth year, that is, until He began the Mission of preaching the Gospel entrusted to Him by His Eternal Father.

7 Q. If families were to live alone, cut off one from the other, could they provide for all their material and moral needs?
A. If families lived alone, cut off one from the other, they could not provide for their individual needs, and hence it is necessary

that they be united in civil society so as mutually to aid one another for the common good and happiness.

8 Q. What is Civil Society?
A. Civil Society is the union of many families under the authority of one head for the purpose of assisting each other in securing their mutual perfection and temporal happiness.

9 Q. Whence comes the authority which rules Civil Society?
A. The authority which rules Civil Society comes from God, who established it for the common good.

10 Q. Are we under any obligation to obey the authority that governs Civil Society?
A. Yes; all who form part of Civil Society are bound to respect and obey authority because that authority comes from God and because the common good so demands.

11 Q. Are all laws imposed by the Civil Authority to be respected?
A. Yes; in accordance with the command and example of our Lord Jesus Christ, all laws imposed by the Civil Authority are to be respected, provided they are not contrary to the law of God.

12 Q. Have those who form part of Civil Society any other duties besides respect and obedience to the laws imposed by authority?
A. Besides the obligation of respect and obedience to the laws, all those who form part of Civil Society are bound to live in peace, and to endeavour, each according to his means and ability, to render that society virtuous, peaceful, orderly and prosperous.

The Commandments of God in General

The Fifth Commandment

1 Q. What does the Fifth Commandment: *Thou shalt not kill*, forbid?
A. The Fifth Commandment, *Thou shalt not kill*, forbids us to kill, strike, wound or do any other bodily harm to our neighbour, either of ourselves or by the agency of others; as also to wish him evil, or to offend him by injurious language. In this Commandment God also forbids the taking of one's own life, or suicide.

2 Q. Why is it a grave sin to kill one's neighbour?
A. Because the slayer unjustly invades the right which God alone has over the life of man; because he destroys the security of civil society; and because he deprives his neighbour of life, which is the greatest natural good on earth.

3 Q. Are there cases in which it is lawful to kill?
A. It is lawful to kill when fighting in a just war; when carrying out by order of the Supreme Authority a sentence of death in punishment of a crime; and, finally, in cases of necessary and lawful defence of one's own life against an unjust aggressor.

4 Q. Does God also forbid us in the Fifth Commandment to do harm to the spiritual life of another?
A. Yes, in the Fifth Commandment God also forbids us to do harm to another's spiritual life by scandal.

5 Q. What is scandal?
A. Scandal is any word, act, or omission which is the occasion of another's committing sin.

6 Q. Is scandal a grave sin?
A. Scandal is a grave sin because, by causing the loss of souls, it tends to destroy the greatest work of God, namely, the redemption; it effects the death of another's soul by depriving it of the life of grace, which is more precious than the life of the

body; and is the source of a multitude of sins. Hence God threatens the severest chastisement to those who give scandal.

7 Q. Why does God, in the Fifth Commandment, forbid the taking of one's own life or suicide?
A. In the Fifth Commandment God forbids suicide, because man is not the master of his own life no more than of the life of another. Hence the Church punishes suicide by deprivation of Christian burial.

8 Q. Is duelling also forbidden by the Fifth Commandment?
A. Yes, duelling is also forbidden by the Fifth Commandment, because duelling has in it the guilt both of suicide and of homicide; and whoever voluntarily takes part in it, even as a simple onlooker, is excommunicated.

9 Q. Is duelling also forbidden when there is no danger of being killed?
A. This sort of duelling is also forbidden, because not only are we forbidden to kill, but even voluntarily to wound ourselves or others.

10 Q. Is the defence of one's honour an excuse for duelling?
A. No, because it is not true that the offence is repaired by duelling; and because honour cannot be repaired by an unjust, irrational and barbarous act such as duelling.

11 Q. What does the Fifth Commandment command?
A. The Fifth Commandment commands us to forgive our enemies and to wish well to all.

12 Q. What should he do who has injured another in the life of either body or soul?
A. He who has injured another must not only confess his sin, but must also repair the harm by compensating his neighbour for the loss he has sustained, by retracting the errors taught, and by giving good example.

The Commandments of God in General

The Sixth and Ninth Commandments

1 Q. What does the Sixth Commandment, *Thou shalt not commit adultery,* forbid?
A. The Sixth Commandment, *Thou shalt not commit adultery,* forbids every act, every look and every word contrary to chastity; it also forbids infidelity in marriage.

2 Q. What does the Ninth Commandment forbid?
A. The Ninth Commandment expressly forbids every desire contrary to that fidelity which husband and wife vowed to observe when contracting marriage; and it also forbids every guilty thought or desire of anything that is prohibited by the Sixth Commandment.

3 Q. Is impurity a great sin?
A. It is a most grave and abominable sin in the sight of God and man; it lowers man to the condition of the brute; it drags him into many other sins and vices; and it provokes the most terrible chastisements both in this world and in the next.

4 Q. Is every thought that comes into the mind against purity a sin?
A. The thoughts that come into the mind against purity are not of themselves sins, but rather temptations and incentives to sin.

5 Q. When is a bad thought a sin?
A. Bad thoughts, even though resulting in no bad deed, are sins when we culpably entertain them, or consent to them, or expose ourselves to the proximate danger of consenting to them.

6 Q. What do the Sixth and Ninth Commandments command?
A. The Sixth Commandment commands us to be chaste and modest in act, in look, in behaviour, and in speech. The Ninth Commandment commands us in addition to this to be chaste and pure interiorly, that is, in mind and in heart.

7 Q. What must we do to observe the Sixth and Ninth Commandments?
A. To be able to observe the Sixth and Ninth Commandments, we ought to pray often and from our hearts to God; be devout to the Blessed Virgin, the Mother of purity; remember that God watches us; think on death, on the Divine chastisements, and on the Passion of Jesus Christ; guard the senses; practice Christian mortification; and frequent the Sacraments with the proper dispositions.

8 Q. What must we avoid in order to preserve ourselves chaste?
A. To preserve ourselves chaste we must shun idleness, bad companions, the reading of bad books and papers, intemperance, the sight of indecent statues or pictures, licentious theatres, dangerous conversations, and all other occasions of sin.

The Seventh Commandment

1 Q. What does the Seventh Commandment, *Thou shalt not steal,* forbid?
A. The Seventh Commandment, *Thou shalt not steal,* forbids all unjust taking and all unjust keeping of what belongs to another, and also every other way of wronging our neighbour in his property.

2 Q. What is meant by stealing?
A. It means taking another's goods unjustly and against the owner's will, that is to say, when he has every reason and right to be unwilling to be deprived of them.

3 Q. Why is it forbidden to steal?
A. Because a sin is committed against justice and an injury is done to another by taking or keeping against his right and will that which belongs to him.

The Commandments of God in General

4 Q. What is meant by another's goods?
A. Everything that belongs to him—everything of which he has the ownership, or the use, or the custody.

5 Q. In how many ways can another's goods be unjustly taken?
A. In two ways: by theft and by robbery.

6 Q. How is theft committed?
A. Theft is committed by taking another's goods secretly.

7 Q. How is robbery committed?
A. Robbery is committed by taking another's goods openly and with violence.

8 Q. In what cases may another's goods be taken without sin?
A. When the owner consents or even when he unjustly refuses. Thus, one in extreme necessity may take another's goods without sin, provided that he takes only so much as is absolutely necessary to relieve pressing and extreme need.

9 Q. Is it only by theft and robbery that another can be injured in his property?
A. He can also be injured by fraud, usury, and any other act of injustice directed against his goods.

10 Q. How is fraud committed?
A. Fraud is committed in trade by deceiving another by false weight, measure and money or by bad goods; by falsifying writings and documents; in short, by deceit in buying and selling or in contracts in general, as well as by refusing to pay what is just and agreed upon.

11 Q. How is usury committed?
A. Usury is committed by exacting, without just title, an unlawful interest for money lent, thus taking an unfair advantage of another's need or ignorance.

12 Q. What other sorts of injustice may be committed with regard to another's goods?
A. By unjustly causing him to lose what he has; by injuring him in his possessions; by not working as in duty bound; by maliciously refusing to pay debts or wages due; by wounding or killing his stock; by damaging property held in custody; by preventing another from making just gains; by aiding thieves; and by receiving, concealing or buying stolen goods.

13 Q. Is it a grave sin to steal?
A. It is a grave sin against justice when the matter is grave; for it is most important for the good of individuals, of families, and of society that each one's right to his property should be respected.

14 Q. When is stolen matter grave?
A. When that which is taken is considerable, as also when serious loss is inflicted on another by taking that which in itself is of little value.

15 Q. What does the Seventh Commandment command?
A. The Seventh Commandment commands us to respect the property of others, to give the labourer fair wages, and to observe justice in all that concerns what belongs to others.

16 Q. Is it enough for one who has sinned against the Seventh Commandment to confess his sin?
A. It is not enough for one who has sinned against the Seventh Commandment to confess his sin; he must also do his best to restore what belongs to others, and to repair the loss he has caused.

17 Q. What is meant by repairing the losses caused?
A. Repairing the losses caused means the compensation which must be made to another for the goods or profits lost owing to the theft or other acts of injustice committed to his detriment.

The Commandments of God in General

18 Q. To whom must stolen property be restored?
A. To him from whom it has been stolen; to his heirs, if he is dead; or if this is really impossible the value of it should be devoted to the poor or to some charity.

19 Q. What should one do who finds something of great value?
A. He should diligently seek the owner and faithfully restore it to him.

The Eighth Commandment

1 Q. What does the Eighth Commandment, *Thou shalt not bear false witness,* forbid?
A. The Eighth Commandment, *Thou shalt not bear false witness,* forbids false testimony in a court of justice, and it also forbids backbiting, detraction, calumny, adulation, rash judgement and rash suspicion and every sort of lying.

2 Q. What is detraction or backbiting?
A. Detraction or backbiting is a sin which consists in making known another's sins and defects without sufficient reason.

3 Q. What is calumny?
A. Calumny is a sin which consists in maliciously attributing to another faults and defects which he did not possess.

4 Q. What is adulation?
A. Adulation is a sin which consists in deceiving another by falsely praising him or others for the purpose of profiting thereby.

5 Q. What is rash judgement or rash suspicion?
A. Rash judgement or rash suspicion is a sin which consists in judging or suspecting evil of others without sufficient foundation.

6 Q. What is a lie?
A. A lie is a sin which consists in asserting as true or false by word or act that which one does not believe to be really the case.

7 Q. How many kinds of lies are there?
A. There are three kinds: The jocose lie, the officious lie, and the malicious lie.

8 Q. What is a jocose lie?
A. A jocose lie is that which is told in jest and without injury to anyone.

9 Q. What is an officious lie?
A. An officious lie is a false statement to benefit oneself or another without injuring anyone else.

10 Q. What is a malicious lie?
A. A malicious lie is a false statement made to the injury of another.

11 Q. Is it ever lawful to tell a lie?
A. It is never lawful to tell a lie, neither in joke, nor for one's own benefit, nor for the benefit of another, because a lie is always bad in itself.

12 Q. What kind of sin is a lie?
A. A lie when jocose or officious is a venial sin; but when malicious it is a mortal sin if the harm done is grave.

13 Q. Is it always necessary to say all one's mind?
A. It is not always necessary, especially when he who questions you has no right to know what he demands.

14 Q. Is it enough for him who has sinned against the Eighth Commandment to confess the sin?
A. It is not enough for him who has sinned against the Eighth Commandment to confess the sin; he is also obliged to retract

whatever he said when calumniating another, and to repair as far as he can the harm he has done.

15 Q. What does the Eighth Commandment command us to do?
A. The Eighth Commandment commands us to speak the truth at the proper time and place, and, as far as we can, to put a good interpretation upon the actions of our neighbour.

The Tenth Commandment

1 Q. What does the Tenth Commandment, *Thou shalt not covet thy neighbour's goods*, forbid?
A. The Tenth Commandment, *Thou shalt not covet thy neighbour's goods,* forbids the wish to deprive another of his goods and the wish to acquire goods by unjust means.

2 Q. Why does God forbid even the desire of another's goods?
A. God forbids the unregulated desire of another's goods, because He wishes us to be just even in thought and will, and to hold ourselves completely aloof from unjust acts.

3 Q. What does the Tenth Commandment command?
A. The Tenth Commandment commands us to be satisfied with the state in which God has placed us, and to bear poverty patiently should God have placed us in that condition.

4 Q. How can a Christian be content in a state of poverty?
A. A Christian can be content in a state of poverty by reflecting that our greatest good is a pure and peaceful conscience; that our true home is heaven; and that Jesus Christ made Himself poor for love of us and has promised a special reward to those who bear poverty patiently.

The Precepts of the Church

The Precepts of the Church in General[9]

1 Q. Besides the Commandments of God what else must we observe?
A. Besides the Commandments of God we must also observe the Precepts of the Church.

2 Q. Are we obliged to obey the Church?
A. Undoubtedly we are obliged to obey the Church, because Jesus Christ Himself commands us to do so, and because the Precepts of the Church help us to observe the Commandments of God.

3 Q. When does the obligation to observe the Precepts of the Church begin to bind?
A. As a rule the obligation to observe the Precepts of the Church begins to bind us as soon as we come to the age of reason.

4 Q. Is it a sin to transgress a Precept of the Church?
A. Knowingly to transgress a Precept of the Church in grave matter is a mortal sin.

5 Q. Who can dispense from a Precept of the Church?
A. Only the Pope, or one who has received from him the power to do so, can dispense from a Precept of the Church.

6 Q. Name the Precepts of the Church.
A. The Precepts of the Church are:
   1. To hear Mass on all Sundays and on Holydays of obligation.
   2. To fast during Lent, on Ember Days and appointed Vigils, and not to eat meat on forbidden days.

---

[9] The current regulations are given after each chapter.

The Commandments of God in General

3. To confess our sins at least once a year, and to receive Holy Communion at Easter each one in his own parish.
4. To contribute to the support of the Church, according to local custom.
5. Not to solemnise marriage at forbidden times, that is, from the first Sunday in Advent until the Epiphany, and from the first day of Lent until Low Sunday.

The First Precept of the Church

7 Q. What does the First Precept of the Church: *To hear Mass on all Sundays and on Holydays of obligation*, order us to do?
A. The First Precept of the Church: *To hear Mass on all Sundays and on Holydays of obligations,* orders us to assist devoutly at Mass on all Sundays and on Holydays of obligation.[10]

8 Q. At which Mass does the Church desire us to assist on Sundays and on Holydays of obligation?
A. The Mass at which the Church desires us to assist, if possible, on Sundays and Holydays of obligation is the Parochial Mass.

9 Q. Why does the Church recommend the faithful to assist at the Parochial Mass?
A. The Church recommends the faithful to assist at the Parochial Mass:
  (1) In order that all the parishioners of the same parish may unite in prayer together with their Pastor, who is their head;
  (2) In order that the parishioners may participate more abundantly in the Holy Sacrifice of the Mass, which is applied principally for them;

---

10 See additional information at the end of each section.

(3) In order that they may hear the truths of the Gospel, which Pastors are bound to explain during Mass;

(4) In order that they may learn the regulations and notices which are published at that Mass.

10 Q. What is meant by the Lord's Day?
A. The Lord's Day means the day of the Lord, that is, the day specially consecrated to divine service.

11 Q. Why in the First Precept of the Church is special mention made of the Lord's day?
A. In the First Precept of the Church special mention is made of the Lord's Day, because it is the principal Christian festival, as the Sabbath was the principal Jewish festival, and because it was instituted by God Himself.

12 Q. What other festivals have been instituted by the Church?
A. The Church has instituted Feasts of our Lord, of the Blessed Virgin, of the Angels and of the Saints.

13 Q. Why did the Church institute other Festivals of our Lord?
A. The Church instituted other Festivals of our Lord in memory of His divine Mysteries.

14 Q. And why have Festivals of the Blessed Virgin and of the Saints been instituted?
A. Festivals of the Blessed Virgin and of the Saints have been instituted:

(1) In memory of the graces which God has given them, and to thank His divine goodness;

(2) In order that we may honour them, imitate their example, and be aided by their prayers.

The Commandments of God in General

The universal law of the Church reckons ten Holydays of obligation: the feasts of Christmas, the Circumcision, the Epiphany, the Ascension, Corpus Christi, the Immaculate Conception, the Assumption, St. Joseph, Sts. Peter and Paul, and All Saints (CIC 1917: Can.1247; CIC 1983, Can.1246). In many countries, by local concessions, they are reduced.

Thus, in the United States the holydays of obligation have been reduced, at the request of the Fathers of the Third Plenary Council of Baltimore, to six days: Christmas, the Circumcision, the Ascension, the Assumption, All Saints and the Immaculate Conception. This discipline is still in force. The solemnity of the Epiphany and of Corpus Christi is transferred to the following Sunday.

The Holydays of obligations traditionally observed in Australia are: Christmas, the Circumcision, the Ascension, the Assumption and All Saints. From December 1st, 1985, the Holydays of obligation are: Christmas, the Epiphany, the Ascension, Corpus Christi, the Assumption, Sts. Peter and Paul and All Saints. When the feast of the Assumption or All Saints falls on a Saturday, no obligation is attached to the feast for that year. The Feasts of the Epiphany, Corpus Christi and Sts. Peter and Paul are transferred to the following Sunday. The current practice is to also transfer the Feast of the Ascension to the following Sunday.

The Second Precept of the Church

15 Q. What is commanded by the Second Precept of the Church in the words, *To fast on the days prescribed*?
A. By the words, *To fast on the days prescribed,* the Second Precept of the Church commands us to observe the fast:
    (1)   During Lent;
    (2)   On certain days of Advent, where this is prescribed;
    (3)   On Ember Days;
    (4)   And on certain Vigils.

16 Q. In what does fasting consist?
A. Fasting consists in taking but one meal a day and in abstaining from prohibited kinds of food.

17 Q. On fast days may a collation be taken in the evening?
A. Through the concession of the Church, a collation may be taken in the evening on fast days.

18 Q. What is the good of fasting?
A. Fasting serves to dispose us better to prayer; to do penance for past sins; and to preserve us from sinning again.

19 Q. Who are bound to fast?
A. Every Christian over twenty-one years of age who is not dispensed, or excused for some good reason, is bound to fast.

20 Q. Are those who are not bound to fast, exempt from all mortification?
A. Those who are not bound by the obligation of fasting are not exempt from all mortification, because all are bound to do penance.

21 Q. For what purpose has Lent been instituted?
A. Lent has been instituted to imitate in some way the rigorous fast of forty days undergone by Jesus Christ in the desert, and to prepare us by penitential exercises to celebrate the feast of Easter devoutly.

22 Q. Why has the Advent fast been instituted?
A. The Advent fast has been instituted to prepare us to celebrate devoutly the Feast of our Lord's Nativity.

23 Q. Why has the fast of Ember Days been instituted?
A. The fast of Ember Days has been instituted:
- (1) To consecrate each of the Four Seasons of the year by some days' penance;
- (2) To beg of God the preservation of the fruits of the earth;
- (3) To thank Him for those already given us;

(4) And to beseech Him to give good priests to His Church, the usual days for ordaining priests being the Ember Saturdays.

24 Q. Why has fasting on Vigils been instituted?
A. Fasting on Vigils has been instituted to prepare us to celebrate the principal Feasts devoutly.

25 Q. What is forbidden on Fridays, and also on Saturdays where not dispensed?
A. On Fridays, and also on Saturdays where not dispensed, it is forbidden to eat meat, except in case of necessity.

26 Q. Why does the Church wish us to abstain from eating meat on these days?
A. In order that we may do penance each week, and especially on Friday, in honour of the Passion, and on Saturdays in memory of the burial of Jesus Christ, and in honour of the Blessed Virgin.

From the Code of Canon Law of 1917, with the modifications approved in 1949, *(complete) abstinence only* is to be observed on all the Fridays throughout the year. *Fast and (complete) abstinence* is to be observed on Ash Wednesday, the Fridays of Lent, Ember Fridays, the Vigils of the Assumption and Christmas, and Holy Saturday. *Fast only (and partial abstinence)* is to be observed on: all weekdays of Lent, Ember Wednesdays and Saturdays, and the Vigils of Pentecost and All Saints.

On the days of fast, only one full meal is allowed. Two other meatless snacks, sufficient to maintain strength may be taken according to each one's needs, but together they should not equal another full meal. Meat may be taken at the principal meal on a day of fast except on the days of complete abstinence. Eating between meals is forbidden, but liquids including milk and fruit juices are allowed.

On holydays of obligation, except in Lent, there is neither fast nor abstinence.

The laws of abstinence binds all who have completed their seventh year of age; the law of fasting binds all persons from the completion of their twenty first year until the beginning of their sixtieth. [The completion of the seventh year means the day after the seventh birthday].

According to the 1983 Code of Canon Law, "All Fridays through the year and the time of Lent are penitential days and times throughout the universal Church. Abstinence from eating meat . . . is to be observed on Fridays throughout the year unless they are solemnities; abstinence and fast are to be observed on Ash Wednesday and [Good] Friday. All adults who have completed their fourteenth year are bound by the law of abstinence; all adults [from age 18] are bound by the law of fast up to the beginning of their sixtieth year." The Episcopal Conference can modify these general rules.

In the United States, "Catholics are obliged to abstain from the eating of meat on Ash Wednesday and all Fridays during the season of Lent. They are also obliged to fast on Ash Wednesday and on Good Friday. Self-imposed observances of fasting on all weekdays of Lent is strongly recommended. Abstinence from flesh meat on all Fridays of the year is especially recommended to individuals and to the Catholic community as a whole."

In Australia, "Abstinence from meat, and fasting, are to be observed on Ash Wednesday and Good Friday. On all other Fridays of the year the law of the common practice of penance is fulfilled by performing any of the following: (a) *prayer*, as for example Mass attendance, family prayer, . . . (b) *self denial*, e.g. not eating meat, not eating sweets or dessert, . . (c) *helping others*, e.g. special attention to someone who is poor, sick, elderly, . . ."

Since a clarity and precision in a law helps for its fulfilment, the faithful are strongly recommended to follow the traditional rules, though only the recent regulations oblige under pain of mortal sin.

The Third Precept of the Church

27 Q. What does the Church command us in the words of the Third Precept: *To go to Confession at least once a year?*
A. By the words of the Third Precept: *To go to Confession at least once a year,* the Church obliges all Christians, who have come to the use of reason, to approach the sacrament of Penance at least once a year.

The Commandments of God in General

28 Q. What is the best time to satisfy the precept of annual Confession?
A. The best time to satisfy the precept of annual Confession is Lent, in accordance with the usage introduced and approved by the whole Church.

29 Q. Why does the Church say that we are to confess at least once a year?
A. The Church uses the words *at least* to let us see her desire that we should approach the sacraments more frequently.

30 Q. Is it useful, then, to go often to Confession?
A. It is most useful to go often to Confession, especially as it is difficult for one who goes only rarely to make a good Confession and to avoid mortal sin.

31 Q. What does the Church command us to do by the other words of the Third Precept: *To receive Holy Communion at Easter, each one in his own parish?*
A. By the words of the Third Precept: *To receive Holy Communion at Easter, each one in his own parish,* the Church obliges all Christians who have come to the age of discretion to receive the Blessed Eucharist every year at Paschal time in their own parish.

32 Q. Are we bound to go to Holy Communion at other times besides Easter?
A. We are also bound to go to Holy Communion when in danger of death.

33 Q. Why is it said that we are to receive Holy Communion at least at Easter?
A. Because the Church earnestly desires us to approach Holy Communion which is the divine food of our souls, not only at Easter, but as often as we possibly can.

34 Q. Is this Precept fulfilled by a sacrilegious Confession or a sacrilegious Communion?
A. This Precept of the Church is not fulfilled by sacrilegious Confession and Communion, because the intention of the Church is that we receive those Sacraments for the end on account of which they were instituted, that is, for our sanctification.

The Fourth Precept of the Church

35 Q. How are we to observe the Fourth Precept: *To contribute to due support of the Church?*
A. The Fourth Precept is satisfied by paying the dues or making the offerings which have been established in recognition of God's supreme dominion over all things and as a means of providing for the becoming support of His ministers.

36 Q. How are these dues and offerings to be paid?
A. They are to be paid in the way and manner customary in the place in which we live.

The Fifth Precept of the Church

37 Q. What does the Church forbid in the Fifth Precept: *Not to solemnise marriage at forbidden times?*
A. In the Fifth Precept the Church does not forbid the celebration of the sacrament of marriage; but only the nuptial solemnities, from the first Sunday of Advent until the Epiphany, and from the first day of Lent until Low Sunday.

38 Q. What are the nuptial solemnities which are forbidden?
A. The nuptial solemnities forbidden by this Precept are the celebration of the nuptial Mass, the nuptial benediction, and marriage festivities on a large scale.

39 Q. Why are marriage festivities on a large scale out of place in Advent and Lent?
A. Pompous displays are out of place in Advent and Lent because these seasons are specially consecrated to penance and prayer.

On the Virtues and Vices

The Main Virtues

Theological Virtues

1 Q. What is a supernatural virtue?
A. A supernatural virtue is a quality infused by God into the soul by which the latter acquires inclination, facility, and promptness to know good and do it towards eternal life.

2 Q. How many principal supernatural virtues are there?
A. The principal supernatural virtues are seven: three theological, and four cardinal virtues.

3 Q. What are the theological virtues?
A. The theological virtues are: Faith, Hope and Charity.

4 Q. Why are Faith, Hope and Charity called theological virtues?
A. Faith, Hope and Charity are called theological virtues, because they have God as their immediate and principal object, and are infused by Him.

5 Q. How can the theological virtues have God for their immediate object?
A. The theological virtues have God for their immediate object, in this way that by Faith we believe in God, and believe all He has revealed; by Hope, we hope to possess God; and by Charity, we love God and in Him we love ourselves and our neighbour.

6 Q. When does God infuse the theological virtues into the soul?
A. God in His goodness infuses the theological virtues into the soul when adorning us with His sanctifying grace; and hence

when receiving Baptism we were enriched with these virtues and, along with them, with the gifts of the Holy Ghost.

7 Q. Is it enough towards salvation, to have received the theological virtues in Baptism?
A. For one who has come to the use of reason, it is not enough to have received the theological virtues in Baptism; it is also necessary to make frequent acts of Faith, Hope and Charity.

8 Q. When are we obliged to make acts of Faith, Hope and Charity?
A. We are obliged to make acts of Faith, Hope and Charity, when we come to the use of reason; often during life; and when in danger of death.

On Faith

9 Q. What is Faith?
A. Faith is a supernatural virtue, which God infuses into our souls, and by which, relying on the authority of God Himself, we believe everything which He has revealed and which through His Church He proposes for our belief.

10 Q. How do we know the truths God has revealed?
A. We know the revealed truths by means of the Church, which is infallible; that is, by means of the Pope, the successor of St. Peter, and by means of the Bishops, the successors to the Apostles, who were taught by Jesus Christ Himself.

11 Q. Are we certain of the truths the Church teaches us?
A. We are most certain of the truths the Church teaches, because Jesus Christ pledged His word that the Church should never be led into error.

12 Q. By what sin is the Faith lost?
A. Faith is lost by denying or voluntarily doubting even a single article proposed for our belief.

The Main Virtues

13 Q. How is lost Faith recovered?
A. Lost Faith is recovered by repenting of the sin committed and by believing anew all that the Church believes.

The Mysteries of Faith

14 Q. Can we comprehend all the truths of Faith?
A. No, we cannot comprehend all the truths of Faith, because some of these truths are mysteries.

15 Q. What are mysteries?
A. Mysteries are truths above reason and which we are to believe even though we cannot comprehend them.

16 Q. Why must we believe mysteries?
A. We must believe mysteries because they are revealed to us by God, who, being infinite Truth and Goodness, can neither deceive nor be deceived.

17 Q. Are mysteries contrary to reason?
A. Mysteries are above, not contrary to, reason; and even reason itself persuades us to accept the mysteries.

18 Q. Why cannot the mysteries be contrary to reason?
A. The mysteries cannot be contrary to reason, because the same God who has given us the light of reason has also revealed the mysteries, and He cannot contradict Himself.

On Holy Scripture

19 Q. Where are the truths which God has revealed contained?
A. The truths which God has revealed are contained in Holy Scripture and in Tradition.

20 Q. What is Holy Scripture?
A. Holy Scripture is the collection of books written under the inspiration of the Holy Ghost, by the Prophets and the Hagiographers, the Apostles and the Evangelists. These books have been received by the Church as inspired.

21 Q. How is Holy Scripture divided?
A. Holy Scripture is divided into two parts, the Old and the New Testament.

22 Q. What is the Old Testament?
A. The Old Testament comprises the inspired books written before the coming of Jesus Christ.

23 Q. What is the New Testament?
A. The New Testament comprises the inspired books written after the coming of Jesus Christ.

24 Q. What is the common name for Holy Scripture?
A. The common name for Holy Scripture is the Holy Bible.

25 Q. What is the meaning of the word *Bible*?
A. The word *Bible* means the collection of holy books, the Book par excellence, the book of books, the book inspired by God.

26 Q. Why is Holy Scripture called the book "par excellence"?
A. Holy Scripture is so called because of the surpassing merit of the content as well as the author who inspired it.

27 Q. Can there be any error in Holy Scripture?
A. There cannot be any error in Holy Scripture since indeed it is inspired by God. The Author of all of the books is God Himself. This does not prevent that in copies and translations that have been made, some errors on the part of the copyists or translators may have crept into it.

The Main Virtues

28 Q. Is the reading of the Bible necessary to all Christians?
A. The reading of the Bible is not necessary to all Christians since they are instructed by the Church; however its reading is very useful and recommended to all.

29 Q. May any translation of the Bible, in the vernacular, be read?
A. We can read those translations of the Bible in the vernacular which have been acknowledged as faithful by the Catholic Church and which have explanations also approved by the Church.

30 Q. Why may we only read translations of the Bible approved by the Church?
A. We may only read translations of the Bible approved by the Church because she alone is the lawful guardian of the Bible.

31 Q. Through which means can we know the true meaning of the Holy Scripture?
A. We can only know the true meaning of Holy Scripture through the Church's interpretation, because she alone is secure against error in that interpretation.

32 Q. What should a Christian do who has been given a Bible by a Protestant or by an agent of the Protestants?
A. A Christian to whom a Bible has been offered by a Protestant or an agent of the Protestants should reject it with disgust, because it is forbidden by the Church. If it was accepted by inadvertence, it must be burnt as soon as possible or handed in to the Parish Priest.

33 Q. Why does the Church forbid Protestant Bibles?
A. The Church forbids Protestant Bibles because, either they have been altered and contain errors, or not having her approbation and footnotes explaining the obscure meanings, they may be harmful to the Faith. It is for that same reason that the Church even forbids translations of the Holy Scriptures already

approved by her which have been reprinted without the footnotes approved by her.

On Tradition.

34 Q. What is meant by Tradition?
A. Tradition is the non-written word of God, which has been transmitted by word of mouth by Jesus Christ and by the Apostles, and which has come down to us through the centuries by the means of the Church, without being altered.

35 Q. Where are the teachings of Tradition kept?
A. The teachings of Tradition are kept chiefly in the Councils' decrees, the writings of the Holy Fathers, the Acts of the Holy See and the words and practices of the sacred Liturgy.

36 Q. What importance must we attach to Tradition?
A. We must attach to Tradition the same importance as the revealed word of God which Holy Scripture contains.

On Hope

37 Q. What is Hope?
A. Hope is a supernatural virtue, infused by God into the soul, by which we desire and expect that eternal life that God has promised to His servants, as well as the means necessary to attain it.

38 Q. What grounds have we to hope that God will give us Heaven and the means necessary to secure it?
A. We hope that God will give us Heaven and the necessary means to attain it, because the all-merciful God, through the merits of our Lord Jesus Christ, has promised it to those who faithfully serve Him; and, being both faithful and omnipotent, He never fails in His promises.

The Main Virtues

39 Q. What are the conditions necessary to obtain Heaven?
A. The conditions necessary to obtain Heaven are the grace of God, the practice of good works, and perseverance until death in His holy love.

40 Q. How is Hope lost?
A. Hope is lost as often as Faith is lost; and it is also lost by the sins of despair and presumption.

41 Q. How is lost Hope regained?
A. Lost Hope is regained by repenting of the sin committed, and by exciting anew confidence in the divine goodness.

On Charity

42 Q. What is Charity?
A. Charity is a supernatural virtue, infused into our soul by God, by which we love God above all for His own sake, and our neighbour as ourselves for the love of God.

43 Q. Why should we love God?
A. We should love God because He is the Supreme Good, infinitely good and perfect; and also, because He commands us to do so, and because of the many benefits we receive from Him.

44 Q. How are we to love God?
A. We are to love God above all things else, with our whole heart, with our whole mind, with our whole soul, and with all our strength.

45 Q. What is meant by loving God above all other things?
A. To love God above all other things means to prefer Him to all creatures, even the dearest and most perfect, and to be willing to lose everything rather than offend Him or cease to love Him.

46 Q. What is meant by loving God with our whole heart?
A. To love God with our whole heart means consecrating all our affections to Him.

47 Q. What is meant by loving God with our whole mind?
A. To love God with our whole mind means directing all our thoughts to Him.

48 Q. What is meant by loving God with our whole soul?
A. To love God with our whole soul means consecrating to Him the use of all the powers of our soul.

49 Q. What is meant by loving God with all our strength?
A. To love God with all our strength means striving to grow ever more and more in His love, and so to act that all our actions should have as their one motive and end the love of Him and the desire of pleasing Him.

50 Q. Why should we love our neighbour?
A. We should love our neighbour for the love of God, because God commands it, and because every man is made to God's image.

51 Q. Are we obliged to love even our enemies?
A. We are obliged to love even our enemies, because they are our neighbours also and because Jesus Christ has made this love the object of an express command.

52 Q. What is meant by loving our neighbour as ourselves?
A. To love our neighbour as ourselves means to wish him and do him, as far as possible, the good which we ought to wish for ourselves, and not to wish or to do him any evil.

53 Q. When do we love ourselves as we ought?
A. We love ourselves as we ought when we endeavour to serve God and to place all our happiness in Him.

The Main Virtues

54 Q. How is charity lost?
A. Charity is lost by each and every mortal sin.

55 Q. How is charity regained?
A. Charity is regained by making acts of the love of God, by duly repenting and making a good confession.

On The Cardinal Virtues

56 Q. Name the Cardinal Virtues.
A. The Cardinal Virtues are Prudence, Justice, Fortitude and Temperance.

57 Q. Why are Prudence, Justice, Fortitude and Temperance called Cardinal virtues?
A. Prudence, Justice, Fortitude and Temperance are called cardinal virtues because all the moral virtues are founded and hinged around them. (in Latin, cardo means hinge)

58 Q. What is Prudence?
A. Prudence is the virtue that directs each action towards its lawful end and consequently seeks the proper means in order that the action be well accomplished in all points of view and thereby pleasing to Our Lord.

59 Q. What is Justice?
A. Justice is the virtue which disposes us to give everyone what belongs to him.

60 Q. What is Fortitude?
A. Fortitude is the virtue which renders us courageous to the point of not fearing danger, not even death, for the service of God.

61 Q. What is temperance?
A. Temperance disposes us to control the inordinate desires that please the senses and makes us use temporal goods with moderation.

The Gifts of the Holy Ghost

1 Q. Name the seven gifts of the Holy Ghost.
A. The seven gifts of the Holy Ghost are, Wisdom, Understanding, Counsel, Fortitude, Knowledge, Piety and the Fear of the Lord.

2 Q. What purpose do these gifts serve?
A. The gifts of the Holy Ghost serve to establish us in Faith, Hope and Charity, and to render us prompt in the exercise of those acts of virtue necessary towards attaining the perfection of a Christian life.

3 Q. What is Wisdom?
A. Wisdom is a gift by which the mind is lifted up from earthly and transitory things, enabling us to contemplate things eternal, that is to say, God Himself, the eternal truth, and to relish and love Him, in which consists all our good.

4 Q. What is Understanding?
A. Understanding is a gift which facilitates, as fas as this is possible to mortal man, the understanding of the truths of faith and of the mysteries of God, which we are unable to know by the natural light of the intellect.

5 Q. What is Counsel?
A. Counsel is a gift by which, amidst the doubts and uncertainties of human life, we are enabled to recognise those things that redound more to God's glory, to our own salvation, and to that of our neighbour.

The Main Virtues

6 Q. What is Fortitude?
A. Fortitude is a gift which inspires us with valour and courage to observe faithfully the holy law of God and of the Church, by conquering all obstacles and all the assaults of our enemies.

7 Q. What is Knowledge?
A. Knowledge is a gift enabling us to estimate created things at their proper worth, and to learn how to use them rightly and to direct them to our last end, which is God.

8 Q. What is Piety?
A. Piety is a gift enabling us to venerate and love God and His Saints, and to preserve a pious and benevolent mind towards our neighbour for the love of God.

9 Q. What is the Fear of the Lord?
A. The Fear of the Lord is a gift which makes us respect God and fear to offend His Divine Majesty, and which detaches us from evil while inciting us to good.

The Beatitudes

1 Q. Name the Beatitudes?
A. The Beatitudes are eight:
  (1) Blessed are the poor in spirit, for theirs is the kingdom of heaven.
  (2) Blessed are the meek, for they shall possess the land.
  (3) Blessed are they that mourn, for they shall be comforted.
  (4) Blessed are they that hunger and thirst after justice, for they shall be filled.
  (5) Blessed are the merciful, for they shall obtain mercy.
  (6) Blessed are the clean of heart, for they shall see God.
  (7) Blessed are the peace-makers, for they shall be called the children of God.

(8) Blessed are they that suffer persecution for justice' sake, for of such is the kingdom of heaven.

2. **Q. Why did Jesus Christ propose the Beatitudes to us?**
A. Jesus Christ proposed the Beatitudes to us to make us detest the maxims of the world, and to invite us to love and practise the maxims of the gospel.

3. **Q. Who are they whom the world calls happy?**
A. The world calls those happy who abound in riches and honours, who lead a pleasant life, and who meet with no occasions of suffering.

4. **Q. Who are the poor in spirit whom Jesus Christ calls blessed?**
A. The poor in spirit are, according to the gospel, those whose hearts are detached from riches; who make good use of riches should they have any; who do not seek them too eagerly, if they have none; and who suffer the loss of such things with resignation when deprived of them.

5. **Q. Who are the meek?**
A. The meek are those who act tenderly towards their neighbour, bear patiently with his defects, and accept the offences and injuries they receive from him without contention, resentment, or vengeance.

6. **Q. Who are they that mourn, yet are called happy?**
A. They that mourn, yet are called happy, are they who suffer tribulations with resignation, and who mourn over sins committed, over the evils and scandals that prevail in the world, over Paradise because it is so distant, and over the danger there is of losing it.

The Main Virtues

7 Q. Who are they that hunger and thirst after justice?
A. They that hunger and thirst after justice, are those who ardently desire to increase daily more and more in divine grace and in the exercise of good and virtuous works.

8 Q. Who are the merciful?
A. The merciful are those who love their neighbour in God and for God's sake, compassionate his miseries, spiritual as well as corporal, and endeavour to succour him according to their means and position.

9 Q. Who are the clean of heart?
A. The clean of heart are those who retain no affection for sin and keep aloof from it, and who above all else avoid every sort of impurity.

10 Q. Who are the peace-makers?
A. The peace-makers are those who preserve peace with their neighbour and with themselves, and who endeavour to bring about peace and concord between those who are at variance.

11 Q. Who are they that suffer persecution for justice' sake?
A. They who suffer persecution for justice' sake are those who patiently bear derision, reproof, and persecution for the sake of the faith and of the law of Jesus Christ.

12 Q. What do the various rewards promised by Jesus Christ in the Beatitudes denote?
A. The various rewards promised by Jesus Christ in the Beatitudes all denote under different names the eternal glory of Paradise.

13 Q. Do the Beatitudes procure us the glory of Paradise alone?
A. The Beatitudes not only procure us the glory of Paradise, but are also the means of leading a happy life, as far as this is possible here on earth.

14 Q. Do those who follow the path of the Beatitudes receive any reward in this life?
A. Yes, certainly; those who follow the path of the Beatitudes do receive a reward even in this life, inasmuch as they enjoy interior peace and contentment, which is the beginning, even though an imperfect one, of the happiness of heaven.

15 Q. Can those who follow the maxims of the world be called truly happy?
A. No, because they have no true peace of soul, and are in danger of being lost eternally.

The Works of Mercy

1 Q. What are the good works, a particular account of which will be asked from us on the Day of Judgement?
A. The good works, a particular account of which will be asked from us on the Day of Judgement, are the works of mercy.

2 Q. What is meant by work of mercy?
A. A work of mercy is a work by which we help our neighbour in his spiritual or corporal needs.

3 Q. What are the corporal works of mercy?
    (1) To give food to the hungry;
    (2) To give drink to the thirsty;
    (3) To give clothing to the naked;
    (4) To give lodging to pilgrims;
    (5) To visit the sick;
    (6) To visit those in prison;
    (7) To bury the dead.

4 Q. What are the spiritual works of mercy?
    (1) To give counsel to those in doubt;
    (2) To teach the ignorant;

The Main Virtues

(3) To admonish sinners;
(4) To console the afflicted;
(5) To forgive offenses;
(6) To bear patiently with persons who are difficult;
(7) To pray to God for the living and the dead.

The Main Kinds of Sins

1 Q. How many kinds of sin are there?
A. There are two kinds of sin: original sin and actual sin.

2 Q. What is original sin?
A. Original sin is the sin in which we are all born, and which we contracted by the disobedience of our first parent, Adam.

3 Q. What evil effects has the sin of Adam brought upon us?
A. The evil effects of the sin of Adam are: The privation of grace, the loss of Paradise, together with ignorance, inclination to evil, death, and all our other miseries.

4 Q. How is original sin cancelled?
A. Original sin is cancelled by holy Baptism.

5 Q. What is actual sin?
A. Actual sin is that which man, after coming to the use of reason, commits of his own free will.

6 Q. How many kinds of actual sin are there?
A. There are two kinds of actual sin: mortal and venial.

7 Q. What is mortal sin?
A. Mortal sin is a transgression of the divine Law by which we seriously fail in our duties towards God, towards our neighbour, or towards ourselves.

8 Q. Why is it called mortal?
A. It is called mortal because it brings death on the soul by making it lose sanctifying grace which is the life of the soul, just as the soul itself is the life of the body.

9 Q. What injury does mortal sin do the soul?
- (1) Mortal sin deprives the soul of grace and of the friendship of God;
- (2) It makes it lose Heaven;
- (3) It deprives it of merits already acquired, and renders it incapable of acquiring new merits;
- (4) It makes it the slave of the devil;
- (5) It makes it deserve hell as well as the chastisements of this life.

10 Q. Besides grave matter, what is required to constitute a mortal sin?
A. To constitute a mortal sin, besides grave matter there is also required full consciousness of the gravity of the matter, along with the deliberate will to commit the sin.

11 Q. What is venial sin?
A. Venial sin is a lesser transgression of the divine Law, by which we slightly fail in some duty towards God, towards our neighbour, or towards ourselves.

12 Q. Why is it called venial?
A. It is called venial Because it is light compared with mortal sin; because it does not deprive us of divine grace; and because God more readily pardons us.

13 Q. Then little account need be made of venial sin?
A. That would be a very great mistake, not only because venial sin is always an offence against God; but also because it does no little harm to the soul.

The Main Virtues

14 Q. What harm does venial sin do the soul?
A. Venial sin:
- (1) Weakens and chills charity in us;
- (2) Disposes us to mortal sin;
- (3) Renders us deserving of great temporal punishments both in this world and in the next.

The Vices and other Very Grievous Sins

1 Q. What is a vice?
A. A vice is an evil disposition of the mind to shirk good and do evil, arising from the frequent repetition of evil acts.

2 Q. What difference is there between a sin and a vice?
A. Between sin and vice there is this difference that sin is a passing act, whereas vice is a bad habit, contracted by continually falling into some sin.

3 Q. Which are the vices called capital?
A. The vices called capital are seven: Pride, Covetousness, Lust, Anger, Gluttony, Envy and Sloth.

4 Q. How are the capital vices conquered?
A. The capital vices are conquered by the exercise of the opposite virtues: Thus Pride is conquered by humility; Covetousness by liberality; Lust by chastity; Anger by patience; Gluttony by abstinence; Envy by brotherly love; Sloth by diligence and fervour in the service of God.

5 Q. Why are these vices called capital?
A. They are called capital because they are the head and fount of many other vices and sins.

6 Q. How many are the sins against the Holy Ghost?
A. The sins against the Holy Ghost are six:
- (1) Despairing of being saved;

(2) Presuming on being saved without merit;
(3) Opposing the known truth;
(4) Envying another's graces;
(5) Obstinately remaining in sin;
(6) Final impenitence.

7 Q. Why are these sins specially said to be against the Holy Ghost?
A. These sins are specially said to be against the Holy Ghost, because they are committed through pure malice, which is contrary to goodness, the special attribute of the Holy Ghost.

8 Q. Which are the sins that are said to cry to God for vengeance?
A. The sins that are said to cry to God for vengeance are these four:
(1) Willful murder;
(2) The sin of sodomy;
(3) Oppression of the poor;
(4) Defrauding labourers of their wages.

9 Q. Why are these sins said to cry to God for vengeance?
A. These sins are said to cry to God for vengeance because the Holy Ghost says so, and because their iniquity is so great and so manifest that it provokes God to punish them with the severest chastisements.

The Last Ends and other Principal Means to Avoid Sin

1 Q. What do you mean by the "last Ends"?
A. The Holy Books call "Last Ends" the last things that will happen to man.

The Main Virtues

2 Q. How many "Last Ends" are there for man?
A. For man there are four Last Ends: Death, Judgement, Hell and Heaven.

3 Q. Why do you say that these are the last things that will happen to man?
A. I say that these are the last things that will happen to man, because Death is the last thing which will happen to him here below, God's judgement, the last judgement that he will have to undergo: Hell, the supreme evil for the wicked; Heaven, the sovereign good for the Just.

4 Q. When must we think about the last Ends?
A. It is well to think of the last Ends each day particularly while saying morning prayer upon waking up, in the evening before retiring for the night and each time we are tempted to commit evil, because this thought is very efficacious to make us avoid sin.

Pious Exercices Recommended for Each Day

1 Q. What must a good Christian do in the morning upon waking up?
A. A good Christian, upon waking up in the morning must make the sign of the cross and offer his heart to God while saying these or similar words: "My God, I give Thee my heart and my soul."

2 Q. What must we think about as we get up and dress?
A. While getting up and dressing, we should think that God is present, that this day could be the last of our life. We must get up and dress ourselves with all possible modesty.

3 Q. Once dressed what must a good Christian do?
A. Once dressed, a good Christian should put himself in the presence of God, kneel in front of a pious picture if he can and

say with devotion: "I adore Thee O My God, and I love Thee with my whole heart; I thank Thee for having created me, for having made me a Christian and preserved me during the night; I offer Thee all my actions and I beseech Thee to keep me from sin during the day and deliver me from all evil. Amen." Next, he recites the "Our Father", the "Hail Mary", the Creed and the Acts of Faith, Hope and Charity; these must be done with an ardent transport of the heart.

4 Q. Which pious practices should be daily accomplished by the Christian?
A. If he can, the Christian should each day:
- (1) Assist at Holy Mass with devotion.
- (2) Pay a visit to the Blessed Sacrament, even if it is a very short one.
- (3) Say the Rosary.

5 Q. What must be done before starting work?
A. Before starting to work, we must offer our work to God and say with all our heart: "Lord I offer Thee this work; give me Thy blessing."

6 Q. What must be the purpose of our work?
A. We must work for the glory of God and to accomplish His Will.

7 Q. What is proper to do before taking one's meal?
A. Before taking one's meal, it is proper to sign oneself while standing and say with devotion: "Lord God, grant Thy blessing on us and on the nourishment we are about to take in order to sustain us in Thy service."

8 Q. After the meal what is proper to do?
A. After the meal, it is proper to sign oneself and say: "Lord, I give Thee thanks for the nourishment Thu hast given us; render me worthy to partake n the Heavenly Banquet."

The Main Virtues

9 Q. What must we do when we are tempted?
A. If we are tempted, we must call upon the Holy Names of Jesus and Mary with Faith or say with fervour some aspirations as for example: "Grant me the grace O Lord never to offend Thee" or to sign oneself with the sign of the Cross. By these external signs we must avoid however that others notice our temptations.

10 Q. When we are certain or that we fear of having committed some sin, what must we do?
A. When we are certain or we fear of having committed a sin, we must immediately say an act of contrition and try to go to confession as soon as possible.

11 Q. When we are outside the Church and hear the bell at the elevation during a solemn High Mass or during benediction of the Blessed Sacrament, what must we do?
A. We must at least in one's heart, make an act of adoration, saying for example: "All praise and all thanksgiving be at every moment Thine."

12 Q. What must we do when the *Angelus* rings in the morning, at midday and in the evening?
A. While the bell rings, a good Christian says the *"Angelus Domini"* with the Hail Mary said three times.

13 Q. In the evening before going to bed, what should we do?
A. Before going to bed at night, it is proper to place oneself in the presence of God as in the morning, to devotedly recite the same prayers, to make a short examination of conscience, and to ask pardon for the sins committed during that day.

14 Q. What will you do before going to sleep?
A. Before going to sleep, I will sign myself, I will keep in mind that I may die that very night and I will give my heart to God saying:"Most Holy Trinity, grant me the grace to live well and to die a happy death; Jesus, Mary, Joseph, I give you my soul"

15 Q. Outside of the morning and evening prayers, what other ways can we have recourse to God during the day?
A. During the day, we can very often pray to God using other short prayers called aspirations.

16 Q. Say some aspirations.
A. "O Lord come to my aid".
"Thy will be done"
"Jesus I wish to be all Thine"
"Jesus mercy!
"Sweet Heart of Jesus, may I love Thee more and more"

17 Q. Is it useful to say many aspirations during the day?
A. It is very useful to say many aspirations during the day, these can also be done simply in one's heart, without saying words, while walking, working, etc.

18 Q. Apart from aspirations what must a Christian often practise?
A. Apart from aspirations, the Christian should practise Christian mortification.

19 Q. What is it to mortify oneself?
A. To mortify oneself is to sacrifice for the love of God what is pleasing to oneself and to accept what is unpleasant to the senses or to self-love.

20 Q. What must we do when the Blessed Sacrament is carried to a sick person?
A. When the Blessed Sacrament is carried to a sick person, we must try if we can to accompany it with modesty and recollection and if this cannot be done we must make an act of adoration wherever we are and say: "Console O Lord this sick person and give him the grace to be conformed to Thy Holy Will and may he obtain eternal salvation."

The Main Virtues

21 Q. What will you do when the bell rings announcing the agony of a dying person?
A. Upon hearing the bell announcing the agony of a dying person, I will go to a church if I can in order to pray for him; if I cannot do so, I will recommend his soul to God, while keeping in mind that before long I will myself be reduced to that state.

22 Q. What will you do when you hear the Toll bell announcing a death?
A. When I shall hear the toll bell announcing a death, I will try to say a "De Profundis" or a "Requiem" for the soul of the deceased and I will renew in myself the thought of death.